SCHOLASTIC
TEACHER BOOKSHOP

Windowsill science

AGES 5 TO 7

LYNNE KEPLER

Adapted from *Windowsill Science Centers* © 1996, Lynne Kepler, published by Scholastic Inc, New York, USA.

Editor
Irene Goodacre

Assistant Editor
Dulcie Booth

Designer
Anna Oliwa

Illustrations
Ann Kronheimer

Cover image
© Stockbyte, © Digital stock
© 2000 John Foxx Images
© Photodisc, Inc

This edition © 2003 Scholastic Ltd

Designed using Adobe Pagemaker

Published by Scholastic Ltd,
Villiers House,
Clarendon Avenue,
Leamington Spa,
Warwickshire
CV32 5PR

Printed by Alden Group Ltd, Oxford

1 2 3 4 5 6 7 8 9 0   3 4 5 6 7 8 9 0 1 2

British Library Cataloguing-in-Publication Data
A catalogue record for this book is available from the British Library.

ISBN 0-439-98358-4

Contents

Introduction

I've always spent a lot of time looking out of windows – wondering about, learning from, and admiring the world just on the other side of the glass. All three of my children have been looking out of windows, too, since they were only a few months old. Even before they could talk, my husband and I would point to falling snowflakes or birds at feeders.

Once the kids began to talk, they started making their own observations and always had plenty of questions! *Why do birds come to our bird feeder? How come all the leaves don't fall? How do the clouds move?* The most-frequently asked question: *What's the weather going to be like today?* usually came in the same breath as: *Can I wear shorts today?* Windows are without a doubt an invitation for learning about what happens in the world and how it directly affects our lives.

So what can the children in your class see outside their classroom window? Do they notice the weather? The colours of the leaves? Birds flying about? A classroom windowsill that acts as a focus for science activities is a wonderful way to involve children in what they are naturally trying to do – understand their world. The activities in this book will involve the children in working with their classmates, talking and listening, writing and drawing, measuring and comparing. And while all of this is going on, they'll develop an awareness of the world outside their window – the kind of awareness that provides a solid foundation for reaching out and understanding the larger world.

Lynne Kepler

Setting up for windowsill science

As you prepare to set up your science windowsill you will probably be asking yourself a few questions:
● How much space do I need?
● Does it matter which way my windows are facing?
● What kind of materials do I need?

A windowsill area about three metres long will provide you with plenty of space. It does not matter which direction the window faces, but you do need to be aware of how this may affect various activities. For activities that require direct sunlight, you may need to make a few adjustments. So, if you are growing plants on your windowsill (see 'Sowing seeds', Chapter 7), you will want to choose plants that suit the light conditions in your classroom.

If your classroom lacks windowsills, consider 'adopting' one. You might be able to 'borrow' a section of windowsill in the school library or the main office. Or think about teaming up with a colleague who does have a classroom with windows. Speaking of teaming up, you could also have windowsill pen pals. This would enable the children to compare the results of their windowsill-based investigations with those of another class down the hall, on the other side of town, or even the other side of the country.

Decorate your windowsill with customised curtains made from old, light-coloured sheets. Let the children decorate the curtains with fabric crayon or paint and add a colourful cardboard valance to ensure you always have a bright and vibrant window.

How to use this book

This book is divided into eight different subject-based chapters with two or three activities in each. All the chapters, with slight variation in the final one, follow the same format to make it easy for you to plan, and allow you more time to focus on the children. The last chapter in the book, 'Windowsill picnic', (page 59), offers a selection of activities that challenge and celebrate the children's learning as they use scientific knowledge to prepare food for a picnic. The activities are presented under the following headings:

Process skills
The process skills that the children will use to explore the concepts developed in the section are listed at the beginning of each one. This information can help you to select areas on which to focus as you guide the children in their work.

Activities
Each section offers several hands-on activities. In most cases, the materials required are simple, inexpensive, and easy to obtain. Step-by-step directions, along with teaching tips, will assist you in guiding the children's investigations.

Science background and vocabulary
Each activity includes a brief explanation of key concepts which you can adapt to meet the needs and abilities of your children. Key science words are also defined, when appropriate, in easy-to-understand language. Look for these in the margins.

Curriculum connections

Curriculum connection activities in each section offer ideas for linking the work you are doing in science with maths, literacy, history, technology and art.

Assessing children's learning

Under this heading you will find ideas for letting the children demonstrate their learning in a variety of ways, but one of the main tools for assessment is the children's own science books. As they participate in the activities, invite them to record observations, thoughts, diagrams, and questions in their books and attach any photocopiable sheets that they have completed. Encourage the children to revisit key concepts by taking time to look through earlier entries in their books.

Window on child development

This provides tips on how the children might perform a skill, or what you can expect them to understand. This information will help you to plan your activities and assessment.

Think about it

How do you know if something is a seed? Why do you think birds have different kinds of beaks? Under this heading you will find questions that you can use to enhance the children's windowsill science experiences. You can adapt both the questions and the answers to suit the children in your class.

Extending the activities

The suggestions here offer ways to expand the children's learning. You might want to let them form co-operative groups to research areas of common interest, then ask the groups to share their discoveries with the class.

Resources

This section offers some suggestions on relevant books, and other resources that will enhance the children's learning experience.

Photocopiable sheets

These sheets (one per section) include 'Windowsill science at home' activities, and data collection sheets for various investigations. Copy and send home page 9 at the start of your windowsill science explorations. You will need to make copies of the others as you work through the different sections.

When you are ready to start your windowsill science investigations, begin with the 'Start-up windowsill science' section that follows (page 7). This provides an activity that will boost the children's observation skills – and inspire them to make new discoveries each time they look out of the window.

Start-up windowsill science

Like photographers looking through viewfinders to capture unusual shots, the children can use viewfinders they make to gain new perspectives on the world around them.

Materials
- blank, unlined index cards (one per child)
- coloured sugar paper (one sheet per child)
- white A4 paper (one sheet per child)
- adhesive or staplers
- hole punch and file reinforcers (optional)
- drawing materials

Steps
❶ Ask each child to make a viewfinder by folding a blank index card in half and cutting a small window (about two centimetres square) in the centre of the card.

❷ Encourage the children to use their viewfinders to focus on a scene outside the classroom window, asking them:
- Can you zoom in on one object?
- Can you hide that object from view and look at something else?
- How do you like the views if you crop out all the sky? If you include the sky?

❸ Ask the children to work in pairs, describing to their partners what they can see inside their frames. Can their partners guess what is being described?

❹ Now ask each child to stick the viewfinder to the centre of a sheet of coloured sugar paper. Demonstrate how to cut out the area of sugar paper that is inside the window of card. (See diagram below.)

❺ Show the children how to place the sugar paper on top of the sheet of A4 paper, then stick or staple the two sheets together along the left-hand side.

❻ Before you go any further, ask the children to share what they saw outside. When everyone has had a chance to contribute, ask them to draw parts of something that they saw inside the framed area of the white paper, then lift the top sheet and draw more of the picture.

❼ When this has been done bring the class together in a circle, encouraging the children to display their framed views and inviting their classmates to guess what they are looking at. Notice whether children were able to capture the idea of looking at just part of something and how well related their guesses are to the parts of the pictures they observe. You may also want to compile the children's drawings into a class big book by punching holes in the margins and attaching file reinforcers.

Year-round windowsill science

As the weather is something the children can observe on a daily basis, it makes a perfect year-round topic, and offers many opportunities for exploration. With a few simple pieces of equipment, such as thermometers and rain gauges, you can turn your windowsill into a weather station where children can collect and record observations about the Sun, clouds, precipitation, wind, temperature, and so on.

Weather diary

Provide a weather diary at the windowsill and give individual, or groups of, children responsibility for recording the information each day. As the children gather and record the data, they'll build a wonderful resource for making all kinds of connections, such as creating graphs, recognising patterns, and developing weather vocabulary. Other ideas for daily weather activities include:

- recording the daily temperature (at the same time each day)
- using pictures and/or words to describe the day's weather
- using pictures and/or words to describe the clouds today
- making a prediction for tomorrow's weather.

Weather words

Be prepared to introduce new weather words to the children as the weather indicates. For example, if the weather report mentions 'gusts of wind' help the children to discover just what a gust is. *I can help – Weather watch* (Franklin Watts) provides weather-based information and activities for young children, while *Weather* by Kay Davies and Wendy Oldfield in the *Starting Science* series offers entertaining facts and things to do.

You could also add to your year-round focus on weather by inviting the children to make a 'weather words' dictionary. Begin by brainstorming a list of weather words, using the weather diary as a reference. Ask the class to put the list in alphabetical order, then choose weather words to define and illustrate. Bind the pages alphabetically with a couple of file reinforcers. Label the first page 'A', the next 'B', and so on, through the alphabet. As the children learn new words, they can create new pages and insert them in the appropriate places.

Windowsill science at home

Dear parent or carer
We've set up a science windowsill in our classroom to explore weather, investigate light, observe birds and grow plants. In all these activities your child will be strengthening lifelong skills such as observing, classifying, predicting, comparing, making conclusions, and communicating. You can help your child to build some of these skills with this activity.

● Ask your child to look out of a window and draw a picture of the view in Window 1. Label the season.

● In the next three windows, invite your child to draw pictures of how the view might look in the next three seasons. Again, label the seasons.

● Follow this up by discussing the changes your child expects to see. For example, how does a tree in summer compare with a tree in winter?

● Display the completed activity page on your fridge door, or a pinboard. As the year passes, help your child to compare these predictions with the seasonal changes.

Window 1 Season _____

Window 2 Season _____

Window 3 Season _____

Window 4 Season _____

CHAPTER 1
Bird detectives

When you work with your class to make and hang up bird feeders, you provide both food for local birds and food for thought for the children. Children are very observant, and will be quick to notice the different types of birds that visit. Watching the birds at their feeders will give them many opportunities to pay close attention to details: the shape and size of birds' beaks, the way they eat, the way they move, the colours of their feathers. This type of observation will help the children to learn more about the ways in which all birds are alike, and how one species differs from another. Birdwatching is also a wonderful way to enhance children's awareness of, and appreciation for, the animals that share our world.

PROCESS SKILLS: observing, predicting, classifying, communicating, comparing, collecting and recording data, making conclusions.

ACTIVITY 1

SCIENCE BACKGROUND
Birds who eat mainly insects, such as **swallows**, often migrate for the winter, although some birds have adapted their diets and will eat any food that is available. When people provide food this helps the birds to conserve energy in winter months when food may be difficult to find. (When birds can find food easily at feeders, they use less energy. This extra energy may then help them to survive extreme weather conditions.)

Different birds prefer different kinds of food. For example, **bluetits** like **seeds, nuts and breadcrumbs**, but **woodpeckers** like **suet**. Once feeders are established they must be kept full during the winter (even over holiday periods) as birds may come to depend on them as a reliable source of food.

Making bird feeders

This activity provides instructions for two simple bird feeders that the children can make by recycling some everyday items. As they prepare their feeders, the children can also put their research skills to work by learning more about birds that are common to their area: *What are they and what types of bird food do they like?*

Note: *The ideal way to observe birds up close is to set out bird feeders near your classroom windows. If this is not possible, then investigate other locations nearby, perhaps a tree near the playground or the school entrance. You could also consider purchasing an inexpensive feeder that attaches to a window with suction cups.*

1: Hanging bird feeder
Materials
For each group:
- a clean, plastic, one-litre soft drinks bottle with cap
- masking tape
- string
- a light, plastic circular lid (perhaps one from a margarine tub; its diameter should be larger than the bottom of the bottle)
- a piece of paper
- birdseed
- the data collection sheet on photocopiable page 17
- writing materials

For teacher use only:
- a craft knife
- a permanent marker pen

Note: *Prepare the plastic drinks bottles by cutting out two triangles from each as shown. To do this, first punch three holes, equally spaced (about one to two centimetres apart) around the shoulder of the bottle, just below the cap. Use a knife to enlarge these holes into small triangles. This is where the seed will come out. Depending on the age of your class, you may also wish to pre-punch two more holes, one centimetre above the bottom of the bottle, on opposite sides, or you might allow the children to do this themselves (see Step 3, below). These holes will be used for threading the string from which the feeders will hang.*

Steps

❶ Before making the feeders, discuss with the class how bird feeders help birds. (See 'Science background', above.)

❷ Divide the class into groups of three. Provide each group with a set of materials: a prepared plastic bottle with its cap, masking tape, a plastic lid, birdseed and a piece of paper.

❸ Ask each group to complete the following tasks:

- Cover the triangular cut-outs with masking tape. (This seals them shut and prevents the seed from falling out before the children are ready to hang their feeders.)
- Thread a piece of string, about half a metre long, through the two holes in the bottle and tie the ends together.
- Trace around the bottle cap on the centre of the lid. (You, or the children, will then need to cut out the cap outline to make a hole in the lid).
- Push the neck of the bottle through the hole in the lid. Make sure that it is a snug fit.
- Use the paper like a funnel to add birdseed to the bottle. Then screw the bottle cap on tightly.

❹ When the bird feeders are ready to hang outside, try to choose branches that are visible, but will not be readily accessible to squirrels. Hang up the feeders and remove the masking tape.

❺ Encourage the children to observe the feeders daily, recording what they see on the photocopiable data collection sheet. (Ask each group to keep a record or allow children to keep them individually.)

2: Suet balls

Materials

- suet (this is beef fat, and should be available from butchers, or the meat department of your local supermarket)
- a large saucepan
- large spoons
- birdseed
- nuts
- breadcrumbs
- a large, empty tin can, perhaps a catering-size coffee tin
- 15-centimetre squares cut from mesh bags (onions or oranges sometimes come in these), one for each child

- 20-centimetre lengths of string, one for each child
- the data collection sheet on photocopiable page 17
- writing materials

Note: *Prepare the suet for this activity by cutting it into chunks and melting in a large saucepan over a low heat. Let the suet cool for a while (but not solidify again) before the children begin the activity.*

Steps

❶ Let the children add the seed, nuts, and breadcrumbs to the melted suet, using the spoons to mix them in.

❷ Carefully pour the mixture into the empty tin can. Leave it to cool until the mixture has solidified. (You may wish to use this time to discuss with the class how the suet changes its appearance as it is heated, and again as it cools.)

❸ Give each child a square of the mesh-bag material and a scoop of the suet mixture. Let them mould the suet into balls and wrap these in the mesh. Demonstrate how to pull the mesh together at the top, twist, and tie it off with string.

❹ Hang the suet feeders in groups from tree branches where children can watch the birds feed, again recording what they see on the photocopiable data collection sheet.

Assessing children's learning

Try to get a sense of the children's attitudes towards other living things by inviting them to draw pictures or write sentences that show how they feel about caring for birds and wildlife.

ACTIVITY 2

Observing birds

Once birds have started to visit the bird feeders, you can focus children's attention on the details they observe. Even by noting just a few details per bird, the children will begin to see the great diversity that exists in the bird world. They will recognise that they share some similar characteristics, but will also see how bird species differ.

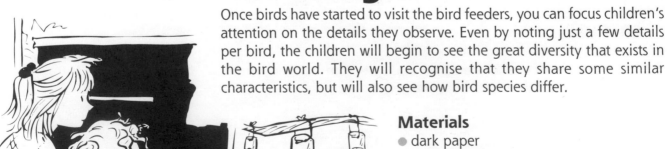

Materials
- dark paper
- masking tape
- a flip chart
- marker pens of two different colours
- paper
- writing materials

Note: *Birds have excellent vision and hearing and this may make it difficult for children to stand next to the windows to observe birds closely. If you can cover a window immediately in front of the feeders with dark paper this will provide a screen between birdwatchers and birds, and allow the children to watch and observe more closely. Cut several slits in the paper for the children to look through and, if possible, make binoculars available, too.*

Steps

❶ Tell the children that they have all just become members of The Great Bird Detective Agency. It is their mission to try to find information that will help them answer some questions. Then use one of the coloured marker pens to write the following questions on the flip chart:

- What colours are the birds you see from the windows?
- Do all the birds you see from the windows visit the feeders?
- Do you think different birds prefer different kinds of food? Why?
- Do the birds that visit eat at the feeders or take the food and eat it somewhere else?
- Can you describe the ways in which the birds you see move?

You could leave the questions displayed on the flip chart or stick them to the paper already attached to the window, above the viewing holes.

❷ Make a set of these questions for the children to keep in their science books and invite them to add some questions of their own. Encourage them to record any information they find that is relevant to the questions in their science books. Call together a weekly meeting of The Great Bird Detective Agency to share information. Record new observations on the flip-chart sheet, using a marker pen of a different colour than that used for the questions.

Assessing children's learning

Before the class begins to observe birds at their feeders, ask each child to draw a picture of a bird, then write or dictate a sentence about the drawing. Collect these and set them aside. Later, once the children have done plenty of birdwatching, ask them to repeat the above task. Compare their drawings and statements and note any changes they have made. *Do your observations show more detail? Have you noticed differences between birds or described bird behaviours?*

Curriculum connection
Making binoculars
(Technology and art)

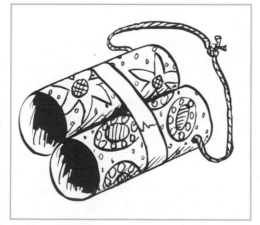

Cardboard tubes (such as the tubes from kitchen paper) can be made into binoculars which the children can use to focus on birds. Each child will need two tubes, masking tape and a piece of string 60 centimetres long. Lay the tubes side by side and tape them together. Help the children to punch two holes on the outside edges of their tubes, then knot one end of the string through each hole. The binoculars could then be decorated with coloured pens or stickers.

SCIENCE BACKGROUND
There are more than 9000 species of birds worldwide and, in addition to learning about local birds, children may enjoy learning some fun facts about other birds of the world. The largest bird is the ostrich, which can weigh more than 130 kilograms and reach heights of two and a half metres. (*How many children equal the weight of one ostrich?*) The smallest bird is the bee hummingbird, which weighs less than 15 grams and is about five centimetres long. (*Can you find things in the classroom that you think weigh as much as a bee hummingbird, then weigh them to find out?*)

Children can research more fascinating facts about birds in nature encyclopaedias and other reference books.

SCIENCE BACKGROUND
Orville and Wilbur Wright are famous for their first flight in 1903 but Leonardo da Vinci was designing flying machines as early as the 15th century. He based his designs on the way that birds' wings move in flight.

VOCABULARY
lift: the force that helps keep flying things aloft, or in the air

Flying lessons

Children should be able to recognise that birds were the inspiration for inventing aeroplanes. In performing this simple experiment they will gain an understanding of the concept of lift, which allows both birds and aeroplanes to stay aloft.

Materials
- three pieces of A4 paper

Steps

❶ A couple of days before you plan to carry out this activity, ask the children to observe birds in flight. Encourage them to record their observations in their science books.

❷ On the day of the activity, invite younger children to move like birds. Ask them to demonstrate how birds flap their wings, how they glide and soar, and even how they land. Older children may prefer to brainstorm a list of action words describing bird flight.

❸ Now ask the children to list any similarities between a bird and an aeroplane. *What do both of these things have that help them to fly?* (Wings.)

❹ Now use the A4 paper to demonstrate the importance of wings. Crumple the first piece into a ball, but leave the second piece flat. (Set the third piece aside for now.) Explain that you are going to drop the two pieces of paper at the same time from the same height. Ask them to predict which piece will reach the floor first.

❺ Once the children have made their predictions, hold both pieces above your head, then release them simultaneously. (The flat sheet will drift back and forth and will reach the floor after the crumpled piece.)

❻ Ask the children to try to explain what they just observed. *Why do you think that the flat piece stayed up in the air longer?* (As the flat piece moves through the air, the air creates lift as it pushes around the paper. Air passing the crumpled paper meets with less resistance and it is therefore able to drop more quickly.) Help the children to make the connection that the wings on a bird and an aeroplane have the same effect as the flat sheet of paper – the air has to push around the wing and, in doing so, it creates lift.

❼ Finally, fold the third piece of paper in half from top to bottom, then allow it to open to form a V-shape. Hold the folded piece and the flat piece of paper above your head and ask the children to describe how they think each piece will fall. Encourage them to explain their reasoning, then release both pieces at the same time. Compare the fall of the two pieces. (Folding the paper helps to equalise the air pressure moving past the paper and creates a more balanced flight.)

Assessing children's learning

Invite the children to apply what they've learned by working in groups to design a set of wings that will stay in the air the longest. *Does the width or length make a difference?* Compare their results with research on birds. For example, the albatross has a wingspan of almost three metres that helps it stay in the air for days at a time.

Window on child development

Even pre-school children can be very adept at identifying the birds they see in their own gardens. However, at this age, it is important to place the emphasis on the birdwatching experience, allowing the children to enjoy the birds they see. Talk about the birds' colours, their beaks, the way they move and encourage the children to describe the birds to you. Some may even create their own names for birds. Once the children are actively involved in observing these bird visitors, they will happily accept the introduction of names such as chaffinch or starling.

Think about it

The children may already be asking questions like those that follow. The explanations are intended for your use, and the information may be adapted to suit the needs and development of your children.

Why do some birds leave for the winter and other birds stay all year?

If you live in a place where the weather gets cold in winter, many birds will leave, or migrate, as winter approaches. Birds that migrate move on to warmer places where they will be able to find food and survive. The birds that remain are ones that have adapted and learned how to find food in the winter.

Why do birds have different kinds of beaks?

The shape and size of a bird's beak is connected to the type of food it eats. For example, birds with long thin beaks, like nuthatches or woodpeckers, use them to poke into trees to find insects.

Why do birds have different kinds of wings?

If you look closely, you will see that birds have wings of different shapes. These shapes typically match the lifestyle of the bird. Many garden birds have broad, rounded wings, designed for manoeuvring through the wooded areas in which they live. Birds such as Canada geese have long, broad wings to help them glide.

Do all birds fly?

Ostriches and penguins are both examples of birds that don't fly.

Extending the activities

● Encourage younger children to be on the lookout for all flying things, keeping a list of anything they observe that flies. Invite them to sort items on their lists in different ways and share their sorting rules with you and their classmates.

● Older children might research the history of flight and develop timelines to illustrate the evolution of flying machines over time.

VOCABULARY

migrate: when animals move from one place to another to find food and shelter

● Investigate the possibility of creating a habitat for birds within your school grounds. Involve the children in all stages – planning, design, and planting.

● If your children become avid birdwatchers you might like to consider becoming involved in the RSPB's Big Garden Birdwatch, a national ornithological study held annually in January. Information and support are provided for families and schools. Some nature-based children's television programmes also organise birdwatching surveys and the children could be asked to look out for information on these.

Resources

Books

How does a bird fly? from the Usborne *Pocket Science* series (Usborne). Simple text and clear photos explain how and why birds fly.

The Usborne Nature Trail Book of Birdwatching by Malcolm Hart and Margaret Stephens (Usborne). How to be a birdwatcher – where to look for, and how to identify, birds.

Other resources

Much information and a range of resources can be obtained from the RSPB UK Headquarters at: The Lodge, Sandy, Bedfordshire, SG19 2 DL or at www.rspb.org.uk.

Data collection sheet

Name_____

Date birds observed	Colour	Beak shape	Behaviour	Food eaten

CHAPTER 2
Shades of green

There are many thousands of different kinds of trees that help to make our world green. In this chapter children will observe trees outside their classroom windows, making discoveries about ways in which the trees are alike and ways in which they are different, noticing how they change with the seasons, and investigating how different structures help trees to survive.

PROCESS SKILLS: *observing, classifying, communicating, comparing, measuring, predicting, collecting and recording data, making conclusions.*

ACTIVITY 1

SCIENCE BACKGROUND

Thousands of different kinds of trees grow all around the world. Scientists typically classify trees into two groups based on their leaves: broad-leafed and needle-shaped. Most broad-leafed trees are deciduous, losing all of their leaves in late autumn. Maple, oak and birch trees are all examples of broad-leafed, deciduous trees. Most needle-leafed trees are evergreens – their leaves remain green throughout the year. Examples of evergreens include pines, firs, cedars, and spruces. Some evergreens, such as hollies and rhododendrons, have broad leaves.

I spy a tree

Do the children recognise ways in which the trees they see are the same, and ways in which they are different? In this game of 'I spy' children enhance their observation skills and learn to differentiate between different types of trees.

Materials
- two pieces of flip-chart paper
- a marker pen

Steps
❶ Play 'I spy' with the children by selecting a tree outside the classroom windows, and giving a very general clue about it. For example: *I spy a tree that is green.*
❷ Write this first clue on one of the pieces of flip-chart paper.
❸ Continue to offer clues until one of the children guesses the correct tree. Record each clue on the chart as you give it. (Alternatively, you may wish to write out the clues before you start the activity and keep them covered, revealing them one at a time.)
❹ Involve the children in a discussion about the clues.
- Which clues apply to more trees than the one I selected?
- Which clues only apply to that one tree?
❺ Ask the children to think of ways in which the trees they see are the same and ways in which they are different. Then draw a line down the middle of the second piece of flip-chart paper, labelling one side 'Same' the other side 'Different'. Fill in any suggestions that the children make. Display the chart and add to it as the children make more discoveries about the trees they see. You could invite them to experiment with other ways to classify the trees and create new charts to show their ideas, for example a chart to compare deciduous trees with evergreen trees.

Assessing children's learning

Ask each child to select two trees and write brief descriptions of these (including where they are located) in their science books. They should also list three ways in which the two trees are the same and three ways in which they are different. (The children may also draw pictures to compare the trees.)

Window on child development

Young children will often draw familiar items in the same way – over and over again. This kind of repetition provides security for the child. Before participating in these activities, the children in your class may draw all trees in the same way – the standard lollipop-style tree. As they make more detailed observations of trees, encourage them to incorporate their observations into their drawings.

Portrait of a tree

In this activity the children select one tree for a long-term study and discover, through their observations, that a tree may look different at different times of the year. Keeping a class diary about the tree will allow the children to look back at the tree over time, make comparisons, and expand their observations.

Materials
- large sheets of paper
- writing materials
- adhesive
- a marker pen
- a camera, with film
- art materials
- treasury tags or ring binder

ACTIVITY 2

SCIENCE BACKGROUND

VOCABULARY
deciduous: trees, such as oaks, that shed their leaves during autumn
evergreen: trees that stay green all year. Some, such as pines, have needle-shaped leaves; others, such as rhododendrons, have broad leaves.

Leaves are only one of the ways in which we can identify trees. Trees are tall plants that typically have a single stem, called a trunk. As the tree grows, new cells are formed within the tree and the dead cells become the bark that protects the inner part of the tree. Bark may be smooth, rough, flaky, dark, or light coloured.

Trees also have different silhouettes or outlines, depending on the species and the growing conditions.

Steps

❶ Let the children choose the tree that they would like to observe. Explain that the whole class will study this one tree for the entire school year.
❷ Take a photograph of the tree, noting the date. Stick this photo to a sheet of paper. (These sheets can later be joined to make a class diary.) Next to the photograph record the date on which it was taken. Choose some children and ask them to collaborate to write a description of the tree on that date. Record this description on the paper under the date.
❸ Try to make sure that the children observe the tree at different times

of day and in different weather conditions. Add a class entry to the diary once a week, if you can. You don't need to take a photo every week, but try to include one periodically, perhaps once a month.

❹ After keeping records for a few months, lead the class in a discussion about the different weather conditions under which they have observed this tree (in a soft summer breeze, in a cold wind, on a frosty morning, on a grey day, under a cloud-filled sky, and so on). Encourage the children to make as many suggestions as they can.

❺ Using the class diary and their own experiences as reference, invite each child to illustrate the class tree under one of the conditions listed. Encourage them to experiment with colour to depict a season or a mood (perhaps using soft yellows to show the Sun's warmth or fresh pinks and greens to represent spring.)

❻ Compile the children's tree portraits into a book using the treasury tags, or by placing the sheets in a ring binder. A cover should also be made and decorated. Encourage the children to add more portraits throughout the year if they wish.

Assessing children's learning

As the children use colour to create moods for their tree portraits, talk with them about how they might portray the tree. *How could you capture changes in daily weather or the seasons?* Talk with the children about the colours they might use for a snowy, rainy, or cloudy day, or a cold day in autumn. *How would your tree look in an early-morning mist?* These conversations between you and the children will help them consolidate their ideas and will help you to determine how much each child understands about how the tree's appearance may change with the weather and the seasons.

Curriculum connection

Tree roots (History)

The children might research and write histories for their tree, beginning with its origins. For example, if they are studying an oak, they will need to find out what an acorn looks like and describe it. Children may also determine the approximate age of the tree – if it isn't too big you may even be able to find someone around school who can remember when it was planted.

Assessing children's learning

Ask the children to write a letter to a friend or relative describing the changing leaf colours of trees they see around the school and their homes.

Evergreen explorations

In this activity the children discover how the leaves of an evergreen help the tree to conserve moisture and withstand harsh weather conditions.

Materials

For each group:
- two paper towels
- one sheet of waxed paper (the same size as the paper towel)
- two paper plates
- water
- the data collection sheet (photocopiable page 24)
- writing materials

Note: *In this experiment, moistened paper towels represent the leaves of different trees. One paper towel, wrapped in waxed paper, represents an evergreen tree leaf. The other, moistened but not wrapped in waxed paper, represents a deciduous tree leaf. Introduce this experiment by displaying samples of leaves from both evergreen and deciduous trees. Let the children touch and compare the leaves. (If you are unable to supply actual leaves, try to provide photos of both kinds.)*

Steps

❶ Explain to the children that in this activity they will be working in groups to find out how leaves help trees to live. Invite them to share their own ideas about this.

❷ Ask each group to:
- wet the paper towels, then squeeze out any excess moisture
- lay one paper towel flat on a paper plate
- lay the other paper towel flat on waxed paper, roll it up (with the waxed paper on the outside), and place it on the second paper plate.

❸ Now ask the children to predict what will happen to each paper towel if it is left out overnight. Let them record their predictions in the first row on the data collection sheet, then set the paper towels aside for the night in a place that does not get direct heat (away from any windows and heat sources).

❹ Next day, let the children check their paper towels and again record their findings, this time in the second row on the data collection sheet. Finally, ask them to complete the third row, where they compare their paper towels with leaves.

SCIENCE BACKGROUND
If you look closely at evergreen trees you will notice a couple of things about their leaves – most are thin and needle-shaped and seem to have a waxy covering. Evergreens developed these adaptations to help them retain moisture. During very cold temperatures or very dry conditions, evergreen leaves resist drying out. You can even tell how cold it is outside by looking at a rhododendron. The lower the temperature drops below freezing, the tighter the rhododendron's broad leaves will curl, helping it to retain moisture. (The leaves will also curl during dry spells in the summer, for the same reason.) Although leaves on deciduous trees fall off, this is also a survival adaptation. When the leaves drop, the food-making process shuts down, helping the trees to conserve energy for the winter.

Assessing children's learning

Allow the children to complete the data collection sheet in their groups, then bring them together to discuss and compare their results. (The paper towel that was not wrapped in waxed paper, representing the deciduous tree leaf, should have dried out first.) Listen to the children's explanations of their results. Can they make the connection between the two paper towels and the kinds of leaves they represent?

If group results are not the same, ask the children what might have caused the differences. (Talk about factors that may have affected results: *Were both paper towels equally moist? Were they both left out in the same place, away from radiators or other direct heat?*) If necessary, repeat the experiment, taking care to control these factors.

Think about it

The children may already be asking questions like those that follow. The explanations are intended for your use, and the information may be adapted to suit the needs and development of your children.

Why are trees important to us?

Trees give us shelter, provide us with shade to withstand heat and wood to build homes. Some animals, such as squirrels and owls, make their homes in trees or use wood from trees to build their homes. Trees also help to supply oxygen to our atmosphere. They also provide beauty and inspiration in our world.

In what ways is a deciduous tree like an animal that takes a long nap in the winter?

As winter approaches and temperatures drop, the leaves on a deciduous tree slowly separate from the tree and die. When the weather warms up, new leaves appear. Losing its leaves actually helps a deciduous tree to survive the winter. If the leaves stayed on, the tree would lose a lot of moisture, and this might cause the tree to dry up and die. Like trees, some animals go to sleep when temperatures drop. This allows them to conserve energy when food supplies are scarce.

Do you think evergreen trees ever lose their leaves? Why?

Individual evergreen leaves eventually die and lose their leaves. Depending on the species, needles can live from two to 25 years. However the leaves don't all die off at the same time so, although you may see brown needles that have fallen off, the tree, if healthy, will still be fully covered with green.

Do you think trees can grow anywhere in the world? Why?
Trees need at least 20 centimetres of rain annually and a summer temperature of at least 10°C to grow. Trees are therefore not found growing in deserts, high in the mountains, or in Antarctica or the Arctic tundra.

Extending the activities
● Children might be interested in creating a field guide of trees around their school. This could then be kept in the school library.
● Consider planting a tree in the school grounds and caring for it. Tending a tree (or caring for any other living thing) is a good way to encourage responsibility and a caring attitude for the Earth.
● Encourage the children to research an individual species of tree, including its physical description, what kind of seed it has, how the seed travels and its possible uses as a natural resource.

Resources

Books
Discovering Trees by Douglas Florian (Aladdin Books). An introduction to trees that includes descriptions of different species, explanations of their life cycle, procedures for telling a tree's age, and ways we use trees.

The Usborne Nature Trail Book of Trees and Leaves by I Selberg (Usborne). Where to find, and how to identify, trees. Also includes sections on how trees grow and what the different parts of a tree do.

Data collection sheet

Name _____

Names of others in my group

_____   _____

_____   _____

_____   _____

	Waxed paper	**No waxed paper**
Which paper towel do you think will dry out first? Why?		
Which paper towel dried out first? Why?		
Which paper towel is more like a leaf on an evergreen tree? Why?		

CHAPTER 3
Tiny worlds

These activities will help the children to gain a greater understanding of the Earth's biosphere – by exploring tiny worlds on their windowsill. However, before beginning this section, you will need to check that you have access to a number of unusual resources!

You will need pond mud and pond water for two of the activities. If you have a pond in or near the school grounds you could visit it, with the children, to collect what you need. If not, ask the children if any of them live near ponds. Make sure that you send a note home explaining what the children are studying and asking parents to accompany their children to the pond to collect any samples. If you cannot find any source of pond water and mud, you can substitute a hay infusion (see Activity 2 on page 27).

You will also need at least one microscope, preferably more than one. The usual educational suppliers will have several models at a range of prices, if your school doesn't possess any.

> **PROCESS SKILLS**: *observing, predicting, classifying, communicating, comparing, collecting and recording data, inferring, making conclusions.*

Under a microscope

Working with microscopes gives the children a chance to use real scientific instruments (like real scientists) to enhance their observations. In this activity, the children make microscope slides in order to take a closer look at the things that they find. From colours in comics to insects that have died, the microscopes will help the children to examine the structure of these things (and you'll quickly discover that they won't want to stop!).

Materials
- a page from a comic (or any other piece of colourful printed paper from a magazine or newspaper)
- paper bags, one per child
- blank index cards (about 10cm by 15cm)
- transparent adhesive tape (the wider the better)
- microscope(s)
- the data collection sheet (see photocopiable page 31)
- writing and drawing materials

ACTIVITY 1

SCIENCE BACKGROUND
The lens of a microscope magnifies or enlarges objects by bending light. Light, on its own, travels in a straight line. The curve of the microscope lens causes the light to bend before it enters your eye, and this makes the object appear to be bigger. The amount of magnification varies, depending on the power of the microscope. A classroom microscope may magnify an object to 30 times its actual size. Very powerful microscopes, used by professional scientists, can magnify images to 100 million times the actual size.

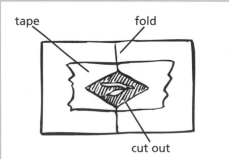

How to make microscope slides.
All you need to make slides are index cards and some transparent adhesive tape. Demonstrate the procedure with the children, following the directions in Step 2.

Steps

❶ Introduce this activity by inviting the children to take turns looking at a section from the comic under the microscope. Before they look, ask them: *What do you think you'll see?* When everyone has had a chance to look, encourage them to compare their predictions with what they saw. (They'll see the structure of the colours – where they see orange in the comic, for example, they'll see yellow and red dots under the microscope. For more information see 'Think about it' on pages 29–30.)

❷ This first experience will make the children eager to look at more samples. Talk about other kinds of things that will (or won't) fit under a microscope, then take a walk outside to collect some samples. Give each of the children a paper bag and explain that they should collect small samples, such as leaves, grass, flower petals, small pieces of tree bark, sand, soil, – basically whatever they can obtain a small sample of (without harming living things) that will fit onto a slide. Let the children use their samples to make several slides each. Show them how to make microscope slides, following these directions:

● Fold a blank index card in half. Cut out a triangle on the fold. When you unfold the card, you'll have a diamond-shaped viewing window.

● Stick a piece of tape over the window on one side only. Place the sample on the exposed sticky side of the tape. Cover the sample with another piece of tape.

● Label each slide, identifying the sample, the person who made the slide, and the date.

❸ Give each child a data collection sheet. Explain that for each slide they should first draw what they think the sample will look like under the microscope. Then, after viewing the sample under the microscope, they should draw what they actually see.

❹ Extend the activity by gathering a new assortment of samples. Make slides yourself, look at them, then draw large pictures of what you see. Number the drawings and assign each slide a letter (keeping a record of which slide letter matches with which drawing number). Display the drawings and ask the children first to guess what each is, then take turns to try to match the slides with the drawings. Some of the children might like to make their own slide-matching games to share with the class.

❺ You are likely to find that the children really enjoy making, and looking at, these slides. They will be keen to swap slides and share their discoveries with their classmates. Encourage the children to bring in other items from home, such as salt, pepper, tea leaves, samples of cloth, onion skins, and so on. They'll discover a whole other world that they have never seen! (and see 'Curriculum connection', below, for a class slide-filing system that the children can set up).

Assessing children's learning

Look carefully at the children's drawings of what they actually see under the microscope. Check that the illustrations show detail that can only be observed through the microscope.

Curriculum connection
Slide-filing system (Literacy)

After the children have made slides with their own samples, suggest that they organise a classroom file. You may want to offer guidance, or you could allow them to decide on their own how to sort and organise the slides. Suggest they start by brainstorming, in groups, possible systems, then bring the class together to share ideas and agree on an approach. (Shoe boxes work well for storage.) Keep the file on the windowsill next to the microscope(s) so that it is accessible to the children.

Making a hay infusion

The world around us is filled with life forms that we can't see with the naked eye. Tiny plants and animals abound in tree trunks, bird baths and puddles. In this activity children use dried grass and rice to create a habitat for living organisms. These will be mostly protozoa, tiny one-celled animals, or microscopic plants known as algae.

Materials
- a large, clear glass jar with a cover (preferably big enough to hold a litre or more)
- hay (a handful of any kind of dried grass from a field or garden will do)
- cooked rice (a few grains of any kind)
- pond mud, puddle water, or stagnant water from a vase of flowers (any water in which life forms are already present, which is just about everywhere)
- eyedroppers
- microscope(s)
- microscope slides with covers
- cotton wool balls
- the children's science books
- writing and drawing materials

Steps
❶ Place a small handful of dried grass at the bottom of the large glass jar. Add several grains of cooked rice and, if you wish, add an inch or two of the pond mud (this will add variety to the assortment of life in the jar).
❷ Fill the jar with the water, then set it on the windowsill, covered, for at least a week.
❸ Ask the children to write a brief description (and/or draw a picture) in their science books of what the jar looks like after it has been put together.
❹ One week later, let the children take a sample out of the jar, using an eyedropper. Show them how to prepare a slide for the drop of water, following the directions below.
  - First wipe the slide with a cotton wool ball (a few cotton fibres will help to slow down the organisms in the water – the fibres get in their way).
  - Then gently squeeze out a drop or two of the pond water onto the slide and cover this with a slide cover.
  - Place the slide under the microscope for viewing. The children can work in pairs so they can discuss their discoveries with a classmate.
Once everyone has had a look, ask the children to draw what they see in their science books. You might want to provide a few reference books so

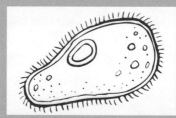

that the children can try to identify the microscopic organisms they find.

❺ Ask the children: *How many different kinds of organisms do you think you spotted? What do you think their food sources are?* Talk about food chains, guiding the children to an understanding that all living things depend on other things for food.

Assessing children's learning

Ask the children to discuss their observations in small groups. Visit each group in turn and listen carefully to their conversations, noting the following points.

● What words do the children use to describe and identify the organisms? Do they use size, shape, and colour words?
● How do they describe the way the organisms move?
● What have they noticed about changes in the jar ecosystem over time?
● What kinds of comparisons do the children make when they are looking at one another's drawings? Do they notice new things?

SCIENCE BACKGROUND

The system that the children create in the jar is much like the various ecosystems found on Earth. Like other ecosystems there is a recycling of gases, such as hydrogen, oxygen, and nitrogen, within the jar. Sunlight comes through the classroom windows and enters the glass jar to provide energy, as it does for other ecosystems. Plants utilise the sunlight to create food for themselves and for other organisms in the system, and consumers and decomposers will live off the energy of the plants. As with any system, there will be changes over time.

Pond in a jar

Create a tiny pond in your classroom so that the children can take a look at life in that ecosystem and, at the same time, learn a little more about what makes other ecosystems on our Earth work.

Materials

● a large, clear glass jar with a lid (preferably big enough to hold a litre or more)
● a nail
● candle wax
● pond water and pond mud
● snails and pond plants (optional)
● microscope(s) and microscope slides with covers
● eyedroppers
● the children's science books
● writing and drawing materials

Note: *Before you start the activity use the nail to punch a hole in the lid of the jar. Seal the hole with melted candle wax. This sealed hole will allow the release of any build-up of gases in the jar.*

Steps

❶ Ask a couple of volunteers to fill the jar three-quarters full with pond water, then add a few scoops of pond mud (to a depth of about three centimetres). If you have any snails or plants add a few of these to the jar as well.

❷ Ask the children to tell you how this pond in a jar is like a real pond. Explain that, like a pond ecosystem, this tiny pond has living organisms interacting with non-living parts of the environment, like water or mud. Let the children sketch the jar in their science books, noting the colour of the water and any organisms they can already see. Ask them to record some predictions of what they think will happen in the jar.

❸ Set the jar on the windowsill and check that the children continue to make and record observations over the next month or two. *What changes do you see? What do you think is causing these changes?* You may wish to take and examine a water sample from the jar every week or two to see if there is any difference in the population of organisms. (You can do this by preparing a slide – see Activity 2, Step 4, on page 27.) As the children gather information, discuss food chains. *Where do you think the plants and animals in the pond get the food they need?*

❹ You might like to enhance the children's ability to think like scientists by inviting them to set up additional jars to investigate any of the following:
- compare an ecosystem set up on the windowsill with one set up in a cupboard
- introduce a pollutant, perhaps a few drops of washing-up liquid, into the system
- find out whether the temperature of the water affects the system
- compare pond water from different ponds.

You could also follow up any suggestions that the children make themselves.

Assessing children's learning

Often the best assessment can be gained from observing the activities that are going on in your classroom. As the children observe the pond in a jar, spend time with them to talk about the records they are keeping in their science books. You could also check their books periodically, recording your own responses to inspire further observations and thought. Questions to guide your assessment of their work include:
- Do their drawings reflect details, such as the size and shape of organisms?
- Do the children record their predictions or make inferences based on their observations?
- Do they show increased use of detail as the entries progress?
- Do they notice changes in the system over time?

Window on child development

Even in their early years children will begin to recognise the concept of a food chain. Most will understand that plants need sunlight to grow, that some animals eat plants and other animals eat plants and/or animals. Young children may have difficulty, however, comprehending that the plants make their own food, therefore the concept of photosynthesis is best left for later years.

Think about it

The children may already be asking questions like those that follow. The explanations are intended for your use, and the information may be adapted to suit the needs and development of your children.

VOCABULARY

ecosystem: the combination of plant and animal communities and their non-living environment. In an ecosystem plants and animals interact with one another and with their environment (food chains are one example of how plants and animals interact with one another).

food chain: a representation of the feeding relationships in an ecosystem where each organism depends on the member below it in the chain for its food. The chain begins with the Sun, which provides energy for plants to grow.

When you look at the comic under a microscope, why do you think you see tiny dots of colour?
The colours we see when we look at the comics are actually made up of tiny dots that are too small for us to see without magnification. When we look at the picture, our brains combine the dots to make new colours – so we see orange, instead of red and yellow.

Why do you think the comics are not just printed with the colours the artist wants us to see?
There are only four colours available in the printing process (magenta, yellow, cyan and black). These can be combined to make virtually every other colour.

How are microscopes helpful to a scientist who studies soil or water? To a person who restores works of art? To a doctor?
Microscopes help scientists to see the things they are looking at in the smallest detail. Thus a scientist studying soil would be able to see what is in the soil; it would help an art restorer to get all the details in a painting just right; and it makes it easier for a doctor to tell what kinds of germs are making us sick.

How do you think the ecosystem in the jar is like the world we live in?
See 'Science background', Activity 3 (page 28).

Where do you think the plants and animals living in the jar get their food?
The plants get their energy from the Sun, the animals feed on plants and other animals.

Extending the activities
● Invite a doctor, scientist, art restorer, lab technician, or another person who uses microscopes to visit the class, bringing with them a high-powered microscope, if possible. Ask the visitor to share how this tool helps with his or her work.
● In the jar pond, children were introduced to food chains. Let them investigate other food chains that exist locally, such as in a field or in a stream.
● Older children might investigate what it is that allows our Earth to support life while other planets in our solar system cannot.

Resources
Books
Habitats: Pond by R and L Spilsbury (Heinemann Library). Looks at the plants, animals, insects and birds that their homes in this ecosystem.

Pond Life by David Stewart (Franklin Watts).

Data collection sheet

Name _____

For each sample you look at under the microscope, draw a picture of what you think you will see in circle 1, then draw a picture of what you do see in circle 2.

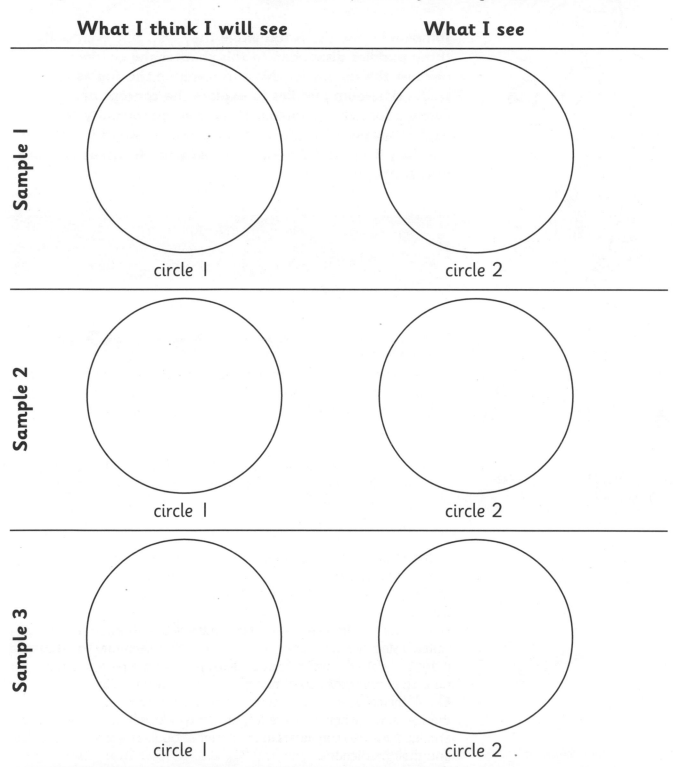

What I think I will see	What I see
circle 1	circle 2

Sample 1

Sample 2

Sample 3

You can use the back of this sheet to draw more samples.

CHAPTER 4
Evaporation investigations

Jumping in puddles is fun while they last, but eventually those puddles disappear. In this chapter the children discover the reason for this and continue the fun as they create classroom puddles to explore the concept of evaporation. The children will have an opportunity to explore evaporation rates, discover how evaporation affects our daily lives, and think about just what happens to those puddles!

PROCESS SKILLS: *observing, communicating, comparing, measuring, collecting and recording data, inferring, predicting, making conclusions.*

ACTIVITY 1

VOCABULARY
evaporation: the process by which water (a liquid) turns into water vapour (a gas)

water cycle: the movement of water from clouds to the Earth, then back to the clouds again

Where does water go?

In this activity the children are introduced to the concept of evaporation and discover the role it plays in the water cycle by observing two jars of water on the windowsill – one open and one covered.

Materials
- two identical clear containers
- a measuring jug
- water
- a permanent marker pen
- cling film
- the children's science books
- writing materials

Steps
❶ Ask two children to fill the two containers with equal amounts of water, using the measuring jug. Invite a couple more volunteers to mark and date the water level on each jar with the permanent marker pen. Then cover the top of one of the jars with cling film.
❷ Ask the children to predict what will happen to the water in each of the containers when they are left on the windowsill. Tell them to draw and label the two containers in their science books, then record the date and their predictions.
❸ Every three to four days ask the children to check the water levels in the jars, marking and dating new levels on the container if necessary.

Each time they do a water-level check they should record the date and their findings in their science books.

Assessing children's learning
After a couple of weeks, ask the children to review their observations by looking back through their science books. *What statement can you make about the water in the two jars?* The water in the open jar seems to be slowly disappearing, or evaporating. Children may have noticed, in the closed jar, that water droplets form on the inside of the cling film and along the sides of the jar. These drops fall back into the water, so the level of the water in the closed jar remains fairly constant.

Puddle races
In this activity the children make (contained) puddles in the classroom and discover that the warmer the location of the puddles, the more quickly the puddles evaporate.

Materials
- eyedroppers (one between two)
- one small jar lid per child (those from baby-food jars are ideal)
- water
- small cups
- flip-chart paper
- permanent marker pens
- thermometers
- the data collection sheet (photocopiable page 38)
- writing materials

Note: *The children need to make one of their puddles on the windowsill, and the other in a place that is cooler than the windowsill. Decide on this location before you start the activity so that the children discover, through the investigation, the reason for the different evaporation rates.*

Steps
❶ Let the children join in pairs for this activity. Explain that they are going to be making puddles in the classroom and invite them to suggest some sensible ways that they could do this. Then share the materials and ask them how they think they could use two jar lids, an eyedropper, and a small cup of water to make puddles.

❷ Demonstrate how to use an eyedropper to make a puddle on one of the lids. Encourage the children to count the drops as you put them in (the number of drops doesn't matter, though you will probably want between five and ten.) Record the number of drops you put in the lid and display this

SCIENCE BACKGROUND
A puddle is made up of water in its liquid state. As water molecules in a puddle heat up, they move faster and farther apart. This allows water molecules to escape into the air and, when this happens, the water molecules are no longer visible. At this point, water is changing from a liquid state to a gaseous state called water vapour. This is the process of evaporation.

Evaporation is just one part of the water cycle. As water evaporates and rises into the atmosphere, it cools and changes into water droplets. This is called condensation. Eventually these water droplets join together to fall back to Earth as rain, snow or some other form of precipitation – then the cycle begins again.

near the windowsill. Ask the children why they think it is important for them all to use the same number of drops. (This is a good opportunity to discuss fair testing. Point out that, by using the same number of drops in each lid, you eliminate the amount of water as a variable when comparing results.)

❸ Tell the children to write their initials on the inside of their lids, then use the eyedropper to make a puddle in each. Show them where to place their puddles (one on the windowsill, one in the cooler location that you have already chosen). Ask the children to label the second location on their data collection sheets, then ask them to record their predictions: *Which puddle will evaporate more quickly – the one on the windowsill or the one in (the other location)?*

❹ Let the children check their puddles every five minutes until one of the puddles completely evaporates, then ask them to complete their data collection sheets.

❺ Create a chart for compiling class results by writing the names of the two locations across the top of a sheet of flip-chart paper. (The children will write their names down the left side.) Display the chart, then bring the children together to share their results. Let each pair of children record their names and put a tick under the location of the puddle that evaporated first. When everyone has recorded their data, ask the children to suggest true statements that can be made about the results, such as: *The puddle on the windowsill disappeared first for all the groups.* Write these statements at the bottom of the flip-chart sheet. The puddles in the warmer, sunnier location (on the windowsill) should evaporate first. If this is not the case, discuss any differences with the children. *Why do you think we didn't all get the same results?* The children might suggest that everyone did not put in the same number of drops. Let them repeat the experiment, if necessary, again recording and comparing the results.

❻ When the children make statements about the results, ask them for possible explanations. Then invite them to suggest ways to prove their explanations. Someone is likely to suggest measuring the temperature of both locations. Provide the children with thermometers to try this out.

Assessing children's learning

The final question on the photocopiable sheet asks the children to think of a way to make a puddle evaporate (children might suggest setting the puddle on something warm, such as a radiator). After they have completed Activity 3, below, ask the children if they can think of another way to make a puddle evaporate more quickly. Then let them test out some of their ideas.

Window on child development

Children's understanding of evaporation and the water cycle develop throughout their early years. Primary-age children will recognise that water in a puddle or in an open container gradually disappears, but they will probably not understand that the water is still present as an invisible gas (water vapour). Children learn to understand these concepts when they are involved in hands-on activities that allow them to make observations, collect information, and draw conclusions about what happens to the water. By revisiting these concepts with related activities, you can build on children's prior understanding and enhance concept development.

Drying laundry

In this activity, children build on what they have learned about evaporation rates by exploring and comparing other variables that can affect drying time.

Materials
- a piece of cloth, such as an old sheet, cut into 12-centimetre squares (you will need two squares per group)
- two clothes lines
- clothes pegs (one per square of fabric)
- hand lenses or microscopes (optional)
- a bowl (or sink) of water
- masking tape
- flip-chart paper
- a marker pen
- the children's science books
- writing and drawing materials

Note: *For the purposes of this activity, the children will need access to a window that can be opened. If this is not possible, investigate other locations in the school, or replace the open window in the experiment with a fan (to represent moving air).*

Steps
❶ Before you begin the activity, hang one clothes line across your opening window and another in front of a closed window. If this can involve your normal science windowsill, so much the better. Clip clothes pegs onto both lines.

❷ Divide the class into small groups and give each group two squares of cloth. Ask the children to use the hand lenses to take a close look at the cloth. You could also invite the children to view the cloth under a microscope, reminding them of the 'Tiny worlds' activities in Chapter 3.

Ask them to use pictures and words to record their observations in their science books, including details of the weave of the cloth.

❸ Now ask the children to submerge their squares in the container of water. While the cloth soaks, review the idea that increased temperatures make water evaporate more quickly. Ask the children if they know of other ways to make something dry more quickly. They may suggest fanning their cloth squares as a way to speed up evaporation. Ask: *How do you think moving air (wind) will affect the drying time of your fabric squares?*

❹ Let each group retrieve two of the wet cloth squares and squeeze out the excess water.

SCIENCE BACKGROUND
In addition to heat, evaporation rates can also vary due to the amount of humidity and wind. Clothes on a line will dry fastest on a warm, dry, breezy day. The type of fabric can also affect drying time. Lightweight items, such as sheets, absorb less water and will dry faster than heavier, more absorbent pieces, such as sweatshirts.

VOCABULARY
wind: moving air

absorbent: able to soak up water

Show them how to hang one square in front of the open window and the other square in front of a closed window.

❺ Let the children check their laundry periodically and record which square dries out first. Then bring the children together to discuss their results. *What conclusions can you make about the best conditions for drying laundry?*

❻ The clothes line can become a semi-permanent feature of your science windowsill and will lend itself to many more evaporation investigations. Children might test and compare drying times of different kinds of fabrics or check drying time against temperature. There are considerable possibilities.

Assessing children's learning
Let the children work together in their groups to brainstorm ways that people deliberately cause water to evaporate each day (hairdryers, tumble-dryers, clothes lines and so on). As children share their ideas, listen to see whether the devices they describe incorporate the concept of evaporation.

Curriculum connection
Fruit strips (Technology)
Before refrigeration people preserved food by drying it. Sailors packed fish and beef in salt to preserve it for long voyages. Challenge the children to apply what they've learned in other evaporation activities by inventing their own food preservers. Provide assorted materials such as boxes, aluminium foil (reflects heat back on the food being dried), tape, string, cheesecloth (to cover the fruit for hygiene), and fruits such as grapes and apples. You could try the following easy recipe as a whole-class activity.

Materials
- 4 cups of strawberries (or any other edible berry)
- a bowl
- a potato masher
- a baking sheet
- cheesecloth (optional)
- waxed paper

Steps
❶ Place the berries in the bowl, and mash.
❷ Spread the mashed berries out evenly on the baking sheet. Protect them by covering them with cheesecloth if you wish.
❸ Let the mashed berries dry. (This will take a couple of days.) Invite the children to select a drying spot, based on investigations in this and other activities, that they think will speed up evaporation.
❹ When the mashed berries are dry, cut the mixture into strips and let the children eat them or roll them up in waxed paper to take home.

Think about it
The children may already be asking questions like those that follow. The explanations are intended for your use, and the information may be adapted to suit the needs and development of your children.

Why are there puddles when it rains?

As rain falls, it collects in lower-lying areas of pavements, roads, car parks and gardens. If the surface on which the water falls is very hot, perhaps the warm tarmac of a car park, the puddle may not get much of a chance to form as the water will evaporate quite quickly.

Where does the water from a puddle go?

As the water in the puddle evaporates, the invisible water vapour rises into the atmosphere. Eventually, this water vapour cools and condenses into a liquid again, in the form of droplets. When many of these droplets join together they form a cloud.

Why doesn't the ocean dry up?

Thanks to the water cycle large bodies of water are constantly being replenished. But rain doesn't taste salty because salt doesn't evaporate with the water. (The children might like to test this.)

Extending the activities

● Before a rain-shower, ask the children to predict where puddles will form. Mark the predicted puddle perimeters with chalk or string and then watch to see where puddles actually do form. The children might also outline puddles that have formed, then observe what happens as the water evaporates.

● Let the children explore water in its three states (solid, liquid and gas). *Can you think of ways to take a cup of water (liquid) and change it into a solid?* (Place it in a freezer.) *Into a gas?* (Heat it up.)

● Challenge the children to find out how changes in the water cycle affect our weather.

Resources

Books

The water's journey by Eleonore Schmid (North-South Books). Clear text and illustrations of landscapes explain the water cycle for young readers.

Where Puddles Go by Michael Strauss (Heinemann). A terrific resource with activities and explanations about concepts associated with the water cycle and other physical changes.

Data collection sheet

Name _____

	Puddle location 1: windowsill	Puddle location 2:
My prediction		
Which puddle evaporated first?		

Why do you think this happened? _____

_____

_____

_____

_____

_____

_____

Can you think of another way to make a puddle evaporate?
On the back of this sheet draw a picture to show your idea.

CHAPTER 5
The way light works

In the activities in this chapter the children will investigate rainbows and explore shadows to discover some of the properties of light. When you are ready to start these activities hang one or two rainbow-making crystals in your classroom window. The children will really love the way these scatter rainbows around the room.

PROCESS SKILLS: *observing, predicting, classifying, communicating, comparing, collecting and recording data, making conclusions.*

Making rainbows

In this activity the children will experiment with a few simple materials to create rainbows in the classroom. By repeating the experiment and by comparing results with one another, the children will discover that the order of colours in a rainbow is always the same: red, orange, yellow, green, blue, indigo, violet. (**R**ichard **O**f **Y**ork **G**ave **B**attle **I**n **V**ain can be a useful mnemonic.)

Materials
For each group:
● a prism
● a pocket-sized mirror
● a clear container (large enough to hold the pocket-sized mirror)

Steps
❶ Ask each group to fill a container with water, then set this on the windowsill in direct sunlight.
❷ Demonstrate how to place a mirror in the water so it is facing the sunlight. Then ask each group to do the same.
❸ Show the children how to adjust the angle of the

ACTIVITY 1

SCIENCE BACKGROUND
Raindrops act as nature's prisms. Light, including sunlight, travels in straight lines. When these light rays are bent, as when they pass through a prism, a spectrum of beautiful colours, called a rainbow, results.

SAFETY TIP!
The first activity requires the children to set out their materials in direct sunlight. This is a good time to remind the children that they should never look directly at the Sun.

mirror until it casts a rainbow. You may wish to place a flat white surface, perhaps a sheet of paper, between the container and the window, to make a surface on which to catch the rainbow.

❹ Allow the groups some time to experiment with their own mirrors to make rainbows.

Assessing children's learning

Observe the children as they try to make their rainbows. Do they adjust the angle of the mirror? Ask the children to describe their rainbows in their science books and to draw pictures of what they see. Do they draw the colours in the correct order?

Colours of a rainbow

In this activity the children discover that they can mix three colours to make six, creating an effect like a rainbow.

Materials
- red, yellow and blue Cellophane
- a brown paper bag
- clear adhesive tape

Note: *Before beginning this activity, cut red, yellow and blue Cellophane into 10-centimetre squares, one square per student. Make sure that there are roughly the same number of red, yellow and blue squares. So, if you have 30 children in your class, cut ten squares each of yellow, red and blue. Place the Cellophane squares in the brown paper bag.*

Steps

❶ Remind the children of the first activity they did in this section (page 39) and the colours made by the mirrors. Ask: *What colours do you see in a rainbow? How do you think we can make those colours from the colours in this bag?* Then ask each child to pick a piece of coloured Cellophane out of the paper bag.

❷ Let the children experiment with the coloured squares, overlaying them on the window to achieve the colours of a rainbow. (One way to do this is to tape the red Cellophane squares to the window first, creating a line of red. Next, tape the yellow Cellophane squares to the window, overlapping by a couple of centimetres with the red Cellophane. Finally, add the blue Cellophane, again overlapping by a couple of centimetres with the yellow Cellophane. When light shines through the Cellophane, a rainbow will form.)

Assessing children's learning

To help the children recognise that the order of colours in a rainbow is always the same, invite them to compare the pictures of their rainbows from Activity 1 with their results in Activity 2. *How are the rainbows the same?*

Shadow graphs

This activity introduces the children to light and shadows by exploring the way light passes through, or is blocked by, different objects.

Materials
- cardboard
- waxed paper
- clear acetate sheets (for overheads)
- masking tape

Note: *Before starting the activity cut a piece of cardboard, a piece of waxed paper, and a piece of clear acetate, each measuring approximately 12 centimetres by 12 centimetres. Tape them in a horizontal row to the wall or board. Next cut about twenty 5-centimetre squares from each of these three materials.*

Steps

❶ Direct the children's attention to the three squares you have taped to the wall. Ask them to predict which of the three will make a shadow when placed in the sunlight.

❷ Allow some thinking time, then ask each child to commit to a prediction by selecting a smaller square made from the same material.

❸ Tape one of each of the smaller squares to the window in a horizontal row, or, for older children, you could prepare labels. See illustration, opposite. Then let the children record their predictions by taping their squares to the window, one above another, in the column with the matching material or the appropriate label. This will form a bar graph representing their predictions.

❹ Then ask the children to notice which squares cast shadows into the classroom. (Ideally, you will be doing this on a sunny day. But if you are not, leave the graph up until you do get some sunshine.) *Which material (cardboard, waxed paper, clear acetate) makes shadows?*

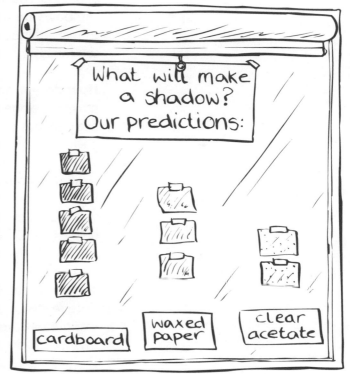

Assessing children's learning

Check that your children understand the concepts in this activity by asking them to make lists of other materials that they think are opaque, translucent, and transparent. Let them work in groups to test out their ideas. Cut out three speech balloons, one for each type of material, and tape them to the windows. Let the children record their discoveries on these speech balloons as they classify the items they test.

Window on child development

When the children sort and group objects, they are classifying. Over time, their classification schemes become more complex. Younger children will simply classify their objects as transparent, translucent, or opaque, but older children can organise their sorting in more detail.

For example, they may be able to arrange the items on a scale of most transparent to most opaque.

Think about it

The children may already be asking questions like those that follow. The explanations are intended for your use, and the information may be adapted to suit the needs and development of your children.

Where do the colours in a rainbow come from?
When light is bent and reflected back, it is always broken into the same spectrum of colours, red, orange, yellow, green, blue, indigo and violet.

Do the colours always appear in the same order?
Yes. The colours always appear in the order of the lengths of each wavelength – from longest to shortest (red to violet).

What do you think would happen if you tried to make rainbows on an overcast day?
One of the ingredients needed to make rainbows is sunlight. On an overcast day, you wouldn't see rainbows.

How do you think changing the angle (position) of the mirror changes what you see?
Whether you see a rainbow or not depends on the angle of the light and how it is reflected back.

How does a rainbow get its shape?
When we see an arched rainbow in the sky, we are actually just seeing part of a perfect circle. The centre of the circle is located below the horizon, leaving just a part of the circle visible to us.

Extending the activities

Children who show special interest in the way light works might like to explore related areas in greater detail. Some suggestions follow:
- explore folklore related to shadows and rainbows
- investigate cloud rays and other light-related phenomena
- research careers where colour is important (perhaps artists, decorators or landscapers).

Photocopiable page 43 provides a simple activity for the children to carry out at home.

Resources

Books

Colour, from the *Step by Step* series (Franklin Watts). Offers activities and simple experiments on colour.

Light and Dark by Wendy Madgwick (Hodder Wayland). Answers questions such as *How are rainbows formed?* and *Why do shadows change?*

Windowsill science at home

Dear parent or carer
We're learning about light in class and you can reinforce your child's understanding by trying this simple activity.
● Look out of a window together after dark tonight. Talk about the lights you see.
● Which are examples of natural light (the moon, stars, fireflies)?

● Which lights come from objects made by people (streetlights, headlights, lights from passing aircraft)?
● Record your discoveries on the chart below. Ask your child to bring the chart back to school by

Natural lights	Other lights

CHAPTER 6
The Sun's warm ways

In the activities in 'The way light works' (see Chapter 5), the children discovered some properties of the Sun's light. In this chapter they explore the heat given off by sunlight so you will want to plan these activities for a sunny day.

PROCESS SKILLS: *observing, classifying, comparing, measuring, predicting, collecting and recording data, making conclusions.*

ACTIVITY 1

SCIENCE BACKGROUND
Light, such as that from the Sun, gives off heat. Heat is a form of energy, and it is the absence or presence of heat that affects temperature – whether something is hot or cold.

Hot spots

In this activity the children will explore the connection between light and heat as they observe differences in temperature between places where sunlight is present, and where it is not.

Materials
- a shoe box
- two (or more) thermometers
- masking tape
- flip chart or board
- sheets of paper for recording
- writing materials

Steps
❶ Set the box upside down on the windowsill. Ask the children to imagine that the box is a hill. *Which side of the box do you think is receiving direct sunlight? Which side is not?* Encourage them to explain their choices.
❷ Now ask the children to pretend that they live on the side of the hill that is in direct sunlight and that they have a friend who lives on the other side. *Will the temperature outside your front door be the same as outside your friend's front door, or is it different?* Again, let the children explain their responses.
❸ Next, ask the children if they can think of any ways to test the temperature on both sides of the hill. If they have been collecting weather data (see 'Year-round windowsill science' on page 8), they may already be familiar with using a thermometer as a tool to measure temperature. Discuss this approach and any other ideas they have before moving on to Step 4.
❹ Guide the children towards recognising that one way to test the temperature is to attach a thermometer to each side of the box. (You can use tape for this.) Ask the children to record the initial temperature on both thermometers, then recheck the temperature on both sides of the hill (box) every 15 minutes for an hour. Record this information on

the flip chart. (Older children may like to create their own charts to record data.)

❺ After an hour, ask the children to look at the data they have collected. *What conclusions can you draw about sunlight and temperature?* (The side in direct sunlight will be warmer than the side that isn't receiving direct sunlight.)

Assessing children's learning

Invite the children to apply what they've learned in this activity by working in groups to make maps of predicted hot spots and cool spots in the classroom. *Which spots do you think will be the hottest? The coolest?* Encourage the children to create simple maps of the classroom, then mark their predictions. Check these to see if they recognise that hot spots will be located in areas of direct sunlight. (If you are doing this activity in the winter, children may predict that areas near heaters will be hot. This is fine, as long as they can explain their reasoning.)

Give the children thermometers to set out at the designated spots and ask them to measure the temperatures every 15 minutes or so for one hour. *How does the data you collect compare with your predictions?* Let the children make new maps showing actual hot spots, or bring the groups together to compile the data and create a map.

Sunlight and surfaces: 1

In this activity, the first of two, the children explore differences in the amount of heat absorbed by materials with different surfaces.

Materials
For each group:
- three small, clear plastic cups (all the same size)
- soil
- water
- sand
- three thermometers
- the data collection sheet (photocopiable page 51)
- writing materials

Note: *Set out the thermometers before you start this activity to allow them to adjust to room temperature. This will ensure that the groups begin the experiments at a similar starting temperature and can later compare their results. (This may be a good time to discuss the concept of fair testing; in this case, having groups start at the same temperature to control the variable of temperature from one group to another.) If you don't have enough thermometers to keep the group size reasonably small, you can let groups take turns over a period of a few days.*

Steps

❶ Divide the children into groups and give each group a set of materials.

❷ Ask each group to fill the three cups – one with water, one with soil and one with sand.

❸ Then ask the children what they think will happen if they set their cups on a sunny windowsill. Discuss their responses. If no one has

SCIENCE BACKGROUND
Smooth and shiny surfaces, like that of water, reflect back much of the Sun's light and, along with it, heat. Darker and rougher surfaces, like those of soil and sand, collect or absorb more of the Sun's light to produce heat.

The colour of the surface also has an effect. Black, the darkest colour, absorbs the most sunlight, making it heat up more than white, the lightest colour, which reflects back all of the sunlight and therefore feels cooler.

VOCABULARY
heat: the kind of energy that make things feel hot or cool

heat absorption: the taking up of heat from the Sun's light by another substance

mentioned that the materials in the cups may heat up, suggest that possibility. (Review the results of Activity 1, in which children discovered that a spot in sunlight will be warmer than a spot that is not in sunlight.)

❹ Next, ask the children to predict which cup will collect (absorb) the most heat. Let them record their predictions in the appropriate space on the photocopiable·sheet.

❺ Now ask each group to check the initial temperature of the contents of each cup and record this information on the data collection sheet. Explain that the children should place the thermometers all the way down into the cups. Discuss the reason for making sure that the thermometers are placed in the same way in each cup (again, the concept of fair testing).

❻ Ask the children to record temperatures for each cup after 30 minutes, and again after one hour, each time recording the temperatures on the data collection sheet.

❼ Once the last temperatures are collected and recorded, let the children, in their groups, work together to draw conclusions about the materials and their heat-absorption qualities. Bring the groups back together to share and discuss their results. (The water will reflect a lot of the light back and will therefore remain cooler. Soil will absorb the most heat because it has a darker surface.)

Sunlight and surfaces: 2

In this activity the children build on what they learned about water, sand and soil in the first part of this work as they investigate the colours of the clothes they wear.

Materials
● sugar paper (you will need at least one sheet of black and one sheet of white plus assorted other colours)
● sheets of paper for recording
● writing materials
● a sheet of flip-chart paper
● thermometers (as many as you have sheets of sugar paper)
● a clothes line and clothes pegs
● masking tape

Note: *Before you begin this part of the activity, string a clothes line across the window area. Cut T-shirt shapes from the black and white sugar paper. Bring the thermometers to room temperature.*

Steps

❶ Ask the children to imagine that they are playing outside on a hot summer day. *What are you wearing? Do you think that the colour of your T-shirt makes a difference to how warm you feel?* Allow them to share their experiences, noting whether some children already appreciate the idea that darker colours absorb more sunlight and therefore feel warmer.

❷ Show the clothes line to the children. Explain that you would like to work together to set up an investigation to find out what colour of T-shirt will help them to feel cooler when they are playing in the sun. Show them that you have already picked out two T-shirts to test (one from a sheet of white sugar paper and one black) and request that they help you make four more shirts. At this point let the children vote for four more colours to add to the investigation. Let them help you cut the paper into T-shirt shapes, using the pre-cut black and white ones as templates.

❸ Involve the children in creating a chart to record the data they collect. They might cut out tiny T-shirt shapes in each of the colours they're testing, stick them down the left-hand side of a piece of flip-chart paper, then make three columns labelled: *Starting temperature*, *After 30 minutes*, and *After 1 hour*.

❹ Help the children to use masking tape to attach thermometers to the back of each T-shirt, then record the initial temperature of each on the chart.

❺ Together, check the T-shirt temperatures after 30 minutes and again after one hour. Record these on the chart.

❻ Ask the children to rank the T-shirts in order, from the hottest temperatures recorded to the coolest. *Based on your findings, which colour do you think would be most comfortable to wear in warm weather?* (The cooler the temperature the better. Generally, white is the coolest and black the warmest.)

Assessing children's learning

Ask the children to draw or write about the type of clothing, including colour, they might wear if they were:
● playing in snow
● playing rounders at a summer picnic.
Let them share their choices with you, explaining how they made their clothing selections.

Curriculum connection

Sandpaper prints (Art)

Show the children how to use the warmth of the Sun in a simple printing process. Start by giving each student a piece of sandpaper, then give them old crayons and ask them to draw coloured pictures on the sandpaper. Encourage them to press hard – something they'll enjoy doing! When they are finished with their designs, let them set the sandpaper pictures on the windowsill in direct sunlight. Ask: *What do you think will happen to your pictures in the sunlight?* Let them find out by observing how the waxy crayon gets sticky as it warms up. When the pictures are warm, let the children press plain white paper over the top of the sandpaper and gently rub, without moving the paper. When the children peel off the paper, they'll have prints of their designs to display around the windowsill.

Keeping heat out

In this activity the children explore the insulating properties of different materials and decide which ones are most effective at maintaining temperature.

SCIENCE BACKGROUND

Insulators help to keep temperatures constant by trapping heat. Remember that heat is not the same as temperature. It is the absence or presence of heat that affects temperature and determines whether something is hot or cold. So an insulated thermos flask keeps a hot drink hot by trapping the presence of heat, and a cold drink cold by maintaining the absence of heat.

Materials

For each group:

- a pint-sized plastic container
- a baby-food jar with a lid
- a thermometer
- cold water
- suitable insulating materials (see Step 1, below)
- flip chart or board
- writing materials

Steps

❶ A few days before you undertake this experiment, brainstorm materials that might help keep something cold from warming up. Record the children's suggestions on the flip chart, then invite them to help you gather up some of the materials on the list. (You might want to send a note home explaining the activity, listing the children's ideas and asking that parents help the children to collect any of the materials that they

can.) Sand, pebbles, soil, newspaper, cotton wool, wool socks (or scraps of wool), foam chips and water are just some of the materials the children might suggest.

❷ On the day of the experiment divide the children into small groups and let each group select one material to test. Make a chart on the flip chart that lists the members of each group and their test material. Leave space to record each group's results.

❸ Provide each group with a pint-sized container, a thermometer, and a baby-food jar with a lid. Then ask the children to follow these directions to test their insulating materials.

- Pour cold water into the baby-food jars. Record the temperature of the water, then screw on the lid.
- Place some of the material you are testing in the bottom of the plastic container.
- Put the baby-food jar inside the plastic container.
- Stuff the test material all around the baby-food jar. Try to fill all the space between the sides of the container and the jar. (If some children are testing wool socks they can wrap a sock around the baby-food jar, then place it in the plastic container.)
- Set your container on a sunny windowsill.

❹ Tell the children that they should check the temperature in their jars every 30 minutes for the next two hours, recording their data on the flip chart. (Confirm that the thermometers have the same starting temperature.)

❺ After this period of time bring the children together to discuss their results.

- How does the temperature of the water in the jar after two hours compare to the initial temperature of the water?

VOCABULARY

insulator: a material that helps to prevent the loss or transfer of heat

● If there is a change, what do you think caused it?

● What conclusions can you make about the ability of each material to stop the heat from the sunlight heating up the cold water?

Based on the sample list provided in Step 1: water, air, soil, sand and pebbles are not good insulators; newspaper, foam chips (and other packing materials) and wool are better insulators.

❻ Follow up the discussion of results by asking why the children think some materials make better insulators (see 'Think about it', below).

Window on child development

Primary-age children are generally not ready to differentiate between heat and temperature. (See Activity 1, 'Science background', page 44). The important thing here is that the children recognise how useful heat is in our lives. Giving them opportunities to connect the idea that light provides heat, and that heat can make something feel warm, will provide a foundation for later learning about heat as energy.

Think about it

The children may already be asking questions like those that follow. The explanations are intended for your use, and the information may be adapted to suit the needs and development of your children.

Do you think the temperature in a sunny spot will be the same in the afternoon as it is in the morning? Why?

Temperatures usually change as the day progresses and the amount of sunlight changes. In discussing this question, the children might be inspired to set up an investigation to test their ideas.

How do you think the temperature on the windowsill compares with the temperature outside?

On a sunny day some of the Sun's light passes through the classroom windows. Once inside, the light is converted into heat and cannot easily pass back through the window, meaning that the heat builds up in the room, making the windowsill warmer.

What colour would you choose to wear to stay warm in winter? Why?

Just as light colours will help keep you cooler in summer (by reflecting back sunlight), darker colours will help you feel warmer in cold weather because they absorb sunlight.

Why do you think it gets so hot in the summer?

In the Northern Hemisphere the Sun's rays are hitting the Earth more directly in summer, resulting in warmer temperatures. Some of this heat is collected by soil and water so that, by the end of summer, they have become saturated and begin to reflect back their stored heat. We sometimes call these late summer days the 'dog days' of summer. This name comes from the ancient Romans who thought that the late summer temperatures were a result of heat coming from Sirius, the Dog Star, which is summer's brightest star.

Extending the activities

● Invite the children to research how solar energy works and what its applications are.

● Investigate the insulators that help keep heat in (or out of) the school, such as curtains, building materials, and so on. The children might follow this up with their families by conducting a similar investigation at home.

● Explore how the angle of the Sun's light affects temperatures and how this is connected with the seasons.

● Learn more about the greenhouse effect, which is related to concepts developed in Activity 1. (Scientists believe that huge quantities of gases in the air are trapping heat and causing changes in the climate.)

Resources

Books

Hot and Cold from the *My World of Science* series (Heinemann Library) by Angela Royston. Clear photographs and simple text support the QCA's Scheme of Work for Key Stage 1.

See for Yourself: Sun by Kay Davies et al (A & C Black). Includes sections on how the Sun helps to ripen fruit and why flowers open in the sunshine.

Heat and Energy by Bobbi Searle (Franklin Watts).

Data collection sheet

Name_____

	soil	water	sand
1. Which cup do you think will collect the most heat?			
2. Which cup do you think will stay the coolest?			
3. Record the starting temperature of each cup.			
4. Record the temperature of each cup after 30 minutes.			
5. Record the final temperature of each cup after one hour.			

Which cup collected the most heat? _____

Which cup collected the least heat? _____

How do your results compare with your predictions? _____

_____

_____

_____

CHAPTER 7

Sowing seeds

Where do seeds come from? What do seeds need to grow? How are seeds like other living things? The windowsill in your classroom is a natural place for year-round plant investigations. As the children plant and tend their windowsill gardens, they'll also develop a sense of responsibility and gain an appreciation for their environment. They will also discover that there are many different kinds of plants – and that these plants serve a variety of purposes.

PROCESS SKILLS: *observing, classifying, communicating, comparing, measuring, predicting, collecting and recording data, making conclusions.*

ACTIVITY 1

SCIENCE BACKGROUND
Children are often surprised to find out that most seeds do not need light to germinate. However, they do need moisture (though not too much), air, and the correct temperature.

Under the right conditions germination will occur. The seed will swell, splitting the seed coat and allowing the roots and tiny leaves to emerge. The length of time it takes a seed to germinate varies from plant to plant and depends on proper conditions. Some sprout after a few days, while others may take two or three weeks.

From seed to plant

In this activity the children plant seeds in clear cups so they can observe what happens when the seeds germinate.

Materials
- clear plastic cups (two cups per child)
- paper towels (one towel per child)
- two or three scarlet runner bean seeds per child (other seeds, such as peas, will work too)
- several shoeboxes with lids
- soil
- string
- strong tape
- the children's science books
- writing materials

Steps
❶ Introduce this activity with a KWL chart. (see 'Assessing children's learning', page 53). Then ask the children to team up with a partner (or in a group of three) and collect their materials. Each team will need four cups, two paper towels and a few seeds.

❷ Demonstrate the following steps, asking the children to copy your actions:
- Pour about one centimetre of water into the bottom of one cup.
- Fold the paper towel in half two times.

- Wrap the folded paper towel around the outside of a second cup.
- Slip this cup inside the first cup. The paper towel should touch the water so that it becomes moist.
- Place the seeds on the paper towel, making sure you can see them through the outside cup.
- Prepare a second pair of cups in the same way.

❸ Before proceeding, ask the children to draw the seed cups in their science books and record the date.

❹ Tell the children to write their initials on their cups (in a spot away from the seeds) then ask each team to place one seed cup in one of the shoeboxes. Replace the lid and set the boxes on the windowsill. The other cups should be placed directly on the windowsill. Note that the seeds in both locations will need to be kept moist. If the paper towels appear to be drying out the children can pour a little water into the space between the outside and inside cups.

❺ Ask: *What do you think will happen to the seeds in each location?* Encourage the children to record any predictions in their science books. Tell them that they should check on their seed cups daily, writing or sketching their observations in their science books. *From your observations, what do you think seeds need to germinate?* Discuss light as a variable in this experiment. *Do seeds need light to germinate?* (No. See 'Science background', page 52.)

❻ When the bean seeds begin to grow out of the cup, the children can remove the inside cup and gently add soil around the seeds in the outside cup. Don't worry about the paper towel. It will begin to break down in the soil and won't be an obstacle for the roots. Let the children water their plants and set them back on the windowsill. Attach string so that it runs vertically from the bottom of the windows to the top (use strong tape to attach the string to the window). Place the plants in front of these strings and show the children how to begin to wind the stems around the string. Soon, you will have scarlet runner bean vines decorating your windowsill!

❼ As an extension to this activity, invite the children and their families to search for seeds in foods at home and then try planting them. (The photocopiable sheet on page 58 is provided for this.)

Assessing children's learning
Seed investigations, like the one described here, present a good opportunity for KWL charts, see picture below. Before starting this activity use one colour of marker to record what the children presently know

WHILE YOU'RE AWAY...
It only takes a little time for seedlings to dry out. If they are left over a weekend on a windowsill, the new seedlings will dry up and die. One way to prevent this is to cover the pots loosely with cling film. Or you could invest in a mini-greenhouse cover, also called a propagator. This is basically a tray for your planters with a plastic domed top and should be available fairly cheaply from garden centres.

about seeds. In a second colour record what it is they would like to know more about. At the end of this activity, and throughout the other investigations in this section, use a third colour of marker to indicate what the children learn about seeds.

What we know	What we want to know more about	What we learned
Seeds germinate	What do seeds need to germinate?	Some seeds don't need light to germinate.

Curriculum connection

Seeds add up (Maths)
Challenge the children to work out how many seeds were planted by the entire class. Depending on the age and ability level of your children, they might simply count (1,2,3…) or they could do some multiplication. (We know that each of us planted two seeds. There are 30 children in our class…)

The children can also keep track of how many seeds germinate. Make a simple chart, perhaps a bar graph, to show how many seeds germinated in each location. Older children might even be able to begin to work out the percentage germination rate for the seeds. This can lead to an investigation of the freshness of the seeds as a variable in germination time. (The fresher the seed, the better the germination rate.) Most seed packets will have a date stamped on them.

Window on child development
Young children are constantly refining their understanding of what an organism is and may not recognise seeds as living things. As they participate in activities that allow them to examine seeds, plant them, and watch them grow, they will begin to recognise the role a seed plays in the lifecycle of a plant. From this starting point the children can begin to understand that one of the identifying characteristics of a living thing is that it grows.

ACTIVITY 2

Greenhouse growing

In this activity the children will discover how warmer temperatures in greenhouses speed up germination.

SCIENCE BACKGROUND
While exploring heat (see 'The Sun's warm ways', Chapter 6) the children discovered that, as sunlight passes through the classroom window on a sunny day, some of that light is converted into heat. This allows heat to build up in the room. Commercial nurseries and keen gardeners use greenhouses to create this effect – maintaining a warm environment for seeds to germinate and plants to grow.

Materials
- three clear plastic cups (for each group)
- mixed birdseed (the kind that contains millet)
- soil
- rulers
- thermometers
- plant spray bottles
- masking tape
- pictures of greenhouses
- the children's science books
- writing and drawing materials

Steps

❶ Divide the children into pairs or threes for this activity. Ask each group to follow these steps:
- Fill two plastic cups with soil.
- Scatter a teaspoon of birdseed over the soil in each of the cups.
- Lightly water both cups using a spray bottle.
- Make a 'lid' for one of the cups by placing the third cup upside down on top of it.
- Tape the cups together. (Even though the cups are taped together, this is not an airtight environment and air will circulate.)

❷ Now ask the children to write brief descriptions or draw pictures of the cups in their science books. Ask them to also record predictions of what they think will happen to the birdseed in both containers.

❸ Tell each group to label their containers and set them on the windowsill. Remind the children to check their cups daily, recording observations in their science books. Demonstrate how to measure and record the temperature of each cup by inserting a thermometer in the soil for five minutes. Make sure that when the children measure the temperature in the covered cups they push the thermometers down far enough that they can replace the lids and so prevent heat from escaping. (After five minutes they can remove the thermometers and replace the lids.)

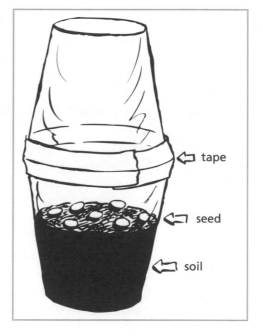

tape

seed

soil

❹ As the birdseed starts to sprout, ask the children to note whether the seeds in the covered or uncovered cup germinate first.

❺ Over the next week encourage the children to use a ruler to measure the length of the plants in each container. *Does the seed in one cup grow more quickly than in the other cup? Why?* Look together at the pictures of greenhouses and discuss how they help plants to grow. Ask the children to identify which of their containers is like a greenhouse.

❻ After several weeks, the children could transplant their birdseed plants to a suitable place in the school grounds or at home.

Note: *You can also use these mini-greenhouses to show the water cycle in action. Draw the children's attention to how the lids of the covered cups are sometimes dry and sometimes clouded with water droplets. Encourage them to try to relate this to their own observations of rain falling, making things wet and then drying up.*

Assessing children's learning

Read the 'The Garden' from Arnold Lobel's *Frog and Toad Together* (see Resources). Ask the children to give Toad's ideas of what he thinks his seeds need in order to grow and list these on the board. Then invite the children to discuss what they now think seeds need to grow (moisture, warm temperatures). Using what they have learned, ask them to compose a letter to Toad or use role-play to give him advice about how he can help his seeds to germinate and grow into plants.

Butterfly gardens

Now that the children have learned what seeds need to start growing, suggest that they grow plants to create a butterfly garden (plants that attract butterflies). You don't need a large plot of land for this. The children can start the seeds indoors and transplant them into window boxes or pots outside if garden space is not available.

Note: *Butterflies and flowers both need warm temperatures, so you need to plan this activity so that the plants flower in early June. Check in advance if there will be a suitable outdoor location for the garden. There are many possibilities – a flowerbed in the playground, a window box, or large pots set in sunny locations.*

SCIENCE BACKGROUND

Butterflies love the warmth of the Sun. It raises their body temperature (they are cold-blooded) so they can fly. It therefore makes sense that, as they visit flowers to feed on the nectar, they prefer ones that grow in full sunlight. Scientists have also discovered that butterflies prefer certain colours of flowers – yellow, pink, purple and white seem to be favourites. Many kinds of flowering plants are suitable – marigolds, snapdragons, sunflowers and zinnias are just a few examples of plants that will attract butterflies to your garden.

You might also like to consider developing some butterflies of your own in a Butterfly Garden – see Resources.

Materials
- a copy of *The Butterfly Seeds* by Mary Watson (see Resources)
- peat pots, paper cups, or egg cartons (with their covers cut off)
- seeds (use some of the varieties mentioned in the 'Science background', opposite)
- soil
- newspaper to cover the work area

Steps
❶ If possible, read *The Butterfly Seeds* – a lovely story about a grandfather who gives his grandson some butterfly seeds to grow.

❷ Follow this by asking the children if they have ever seen butterflies on a plant. *Did you notice anything special about these plants?* Suggest that butterflies like plants with flowers and share some of the information from the 'Science background' above about the kinds of plants that butterflies prefer.

❸ Now invite the children to start their own butterfly garden on the windowsill. Set out peat pots (or other containers), soil and 'butterfly seeds' for the children to plant. (You might want to provide enough materials for children to plant two pots each – one to leave at school and one to take home.) Before the children begin planting, review what they know about the things that seeds and plants need in order to grow.

❹ Check that the children have planted and watered the seeds as directed on the packets, then set the pots on the windowsill. Once the plants are well established, let the children transplant them to a suitable location outdoors – in the ground, in pots or in window boxes. Plants in peat pots can be planted directly into the soil, but if children have used paper cups they will need to peel away the paper from the plants.

Assessing children's learning
Make a photo diary of the butterfly garden project, taking pictures of your young scientists tending their gardens. Let the children add captions to the photos to show what they have observed. You can focus children's

responses and help them reveal what they learned in greater depth and detail by providing prompts for various pictures. You can do this by attaching questions to photos. For example, next to a photo of a seedling you can ask: *What are two things this seedling needs to grow?*

Think about it
The children may already be asking questions like those that follow. The explanations are intended for your use, and the information may be adapted to suit the needs and development of your children.

How do you know if something is a seed?
Inside every seed is a young plant called an embryo. Given the proper conditions, a seed can germinate and grow into a plant.

In what ways are seeds are like other living things?
Like other living things, seeds need food and water; they grow and develop; and they reproduce themselves.

Where do seeds come from?
Flowering plants and cone-bearing trees produce seeds. Parts of the flower work together to produce seeds. This includes the fruit, which serves to protect the seeds. When the seeds are ready, the fruit ripens and the seeds disperse, continuing the plant's lifecycle.

Extending the activities
Challenge the children to investigate how seeds disperse or how soil types affect plant growth.

Resources

Books
The Butterfly Seeds by Mary Watson (William Morrow). A grandfather gives his grandson 'butterfly seeds' to take to America. The boy plants the seeds in an old crate that he turns into a window box and waits for the butterflies to arrive.

Frog and Toad Together by Arnold Lobel (Mammoth). There are several wonderful short stories in this book. One story, entitled 'The Garden', finds Toad worried about his seeds and determined to make them sprout by shouting at them and playing music for the seeds to hear.

The *Take Off* series by Angela Royston (Heinemann) includes a number of useful titles on plants such as: *Flowers, Fruits and Seeds* or *How Plants Grow*.

Other resources
The Butterfly Garden is a kit that comes with live caterpillars and instructions on how to rear them. It is available from Insect Lore, PO Box 1420, Kiln Farm, Milton Keynes, MK19 6ZH or www.insectlore-europe.com. This company supplies a range of lovely nature-based resources for young children.

WHAT'S A PEAT POT?
Peat pots are handy for germinating seeds. They're small containers sometimes connected to one another, like egg cartons. They're made from peat and, when the seedlings are ready for transplanting, the pots can be put directly into the soil (they will break down). Peat pots are inexpensive and are available in garden centres.

MORE THEMED GARDENS TO GROW
Pizza garden: tomatoes, oregano, basil and chives.
Senses garden: mint (smell), fennel (taste), marigolds (sight), gourds (sound), lamb's ears (touch).
Alphabet garden: A for aster, B for beans, C for cress and so on.

Windowsill science at home

Dear parent or carer

As part of our work in science we are germinating seeds and growing plants to find out what seeds and plants need to grow. You can enrich your child's understanding about seeds with this activity. It doesn't take long, it is great fun – and you can do it while you're enjoying your breakfast or dinner! Here's what to do:

1. When you and your child are preparing or eating a meal, try to spot seeds in some of the foods, such as beans, cucumbers, melons or sugarsnap peas.

2. When you find seeds, place them on a paper towel to dry. Write each seed's name next to it.

3. Select some seeds to plant together. Just follow these steps:

- You'll need a paper cup (egg cartons work well too) and some soil to germinate the seeds.
- Plant each seed about ½ centimetre under the soil (one or two per cup or egg carton cup). Moisten the soil and place the container(s) in a warm sunny spot (but not too near a heater).

- Invite your child to draw a picture of what the seeds might look like when they sprout. Ask too how many days they think it will take for the seeds to sprout.

Thank you for working on this science activity with your child.

CHAPTER 8
Windowsill picnic

This collection of activities celebrates the children's ongoing learning from their windowsill science. From discovering how the Sun provides light and warmth to recognising what seeds need to grow, the children will apply what they've learned in preparing a picnic to share. They'll employ their knowledge of evaporation as they use the Sun's heat to dry apples. They'll also use the Sun to steep tea and make bread dough (and discover that tiny organisms – like yeast – don't just live in ponds). They'll also germinate mustard and cress seeds to enjoy.

PROCESS SKILLS: *observing, communicating, comparing, predicting, measuring, collecting and recording data, making conclusions.*

Sprouting seeds

About one week before the picnic, let the children apply their seed-germinating skills to grow some mustard and cress.

Materials
- self-sealing plastic sandwich bags (one bag per group)
- mustard and cress seeds (radish, mung beans and other sprouting seeds are also possibilities)
- a hole-punch
- a permanent marker pen
- a large bowl (or sinkful) of water
- string (one 25-centimetre piece of string for each group)
- the clothes line created for 'Drying laundry' (see page 35) hung in a dark place like a cupboard
- clothes pegs

Note: *Just before the activity, fill a bowl with warm water and set it on the windowsill.*

Steps
❶ Ask the children to work in small groups to prepare the seeds. Take them through the following steps:
- Cut three small triangles out of the bottom of the plastic sandwich bag. This will provide drainage for the water.
- Use the hole-punch to make a hole just under the seal of the bag.
- Write the initials of the group members on the bag with the marker pen.

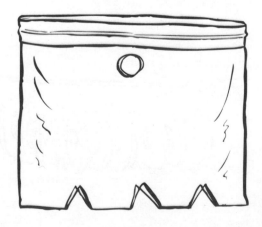

SCIENCE BACKGROUND
Plants make up an important part of our diets. When we eat plants, we may be eating fruits, roots, flowers, leaves, or seeds. Tomatoes and apples are fruits. Carrots and potatoes are roots. Spinach is made up of leaves and broccoli is made up of flowers. Peas and beans are seeds. In this activity the children will be planting seeds that germinate quickly – with mustard and cress ready for eating in just a few days.

● Add a small handful of seeds to the bag.

● Seal the bag and place it in the bowl of warm water. Leave the bags in the bowl overnight.

❷ Next morning, ask one child from each group to hold the bag over the bowl until all the water has drained from the bag. Help the children to run a piece of string through the holes in the bags and hang them on the clothes line. Leave them in the cupboard for a couple of days. Explain that this is where the seeds will germinate.

❸ Ask the children how many days they think it will take for the seeds to germinate. Record their guesses.

❹ Tell the children to check the seeds daily and record their observations. They should also spray the seeds with water once or twice a day to keep them moist.

❺ Once the seeds have sprouted (probably three to five days), hang the bags above the windowsill (from the clothes line). After several days they will be green and ready to eat, either as they are, or as part of a sandwich filling.

Assessing children's learning

Ask the children to write or draw directions, on cards, for growing sprouting seeds. Attach their cards to small bags of seeds that they can take home.

Curriculum connection

Classifying foods (Maths and Literacy)

Share the 'Science background' (above) with the children. Then brainstorm fruits and vegetables that they eat, recording their contributions on a flip chart or board.

Ask younger children to cut out pictures of some of these foods from magazines. Then place the pictures on a tray and invite them to work with partners to classify the foods. *Can you find foods that are flowers? Roots? Leaves? Fruits? Seeds?* You might like to make sorting mats for each category, including a sample picture of each.

Older children could be asked to keep a record of the flowers, roots, leaves, fruits and seeds in their diets.

Drying apples (Technology and Maths)

For hundreds of years, people have preserved food by drying it. Drying food eliminates the moisture that can cause mould to grow and food to spoil. Let children discover how evaporation helps dry and preserve food by making dried apple rings. Follow these simple directions:

● About a week before your picnic, peel and core some apples and slice them into rings. Ask the children to predict how much the apples weigh now and how much they will weigh after they dry. Weigh the apples and record the weight.

● Let the children work together to string the apple rings. Use clothes pegs to attach the string of apple rings to the clothes line at your windowsill, making sure the slices don't touch one another.

● Drape cheesecloth over the apples to keep dust and flies off the fruit. Then observe what happens to the apples. (They'll shrink in size and wrinkle as the water in

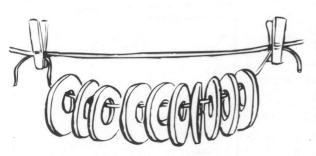

them evaporates). *Where does the water go?* (It turns into water vapour.)
● Once the apple rings have dried, weigh them again. *What do you think has caused the change in weight?* (Loss of water.) Enjoy the apple rings at your picnic!

Rising bread

While making bread for the windowsill picnic, the children will learn how yeast, a single-celled organism, and warm air, help dough to rise. You can make the dough the day before or start it the morning of the picnic.

Materials
● the ingredients for bread dough (see below)
● one sachet of active dry yeast (in addition to the two sachets needed for the bread)
● two baby-food jars
● measuring cups and spoons
● two large bowls
● waxed paper (to cover the table or work area)
● cooking oil
● two wooden spoons
● a ruler

Bread ingredients
● 2 sachets of active dry yeast (check the date to make sure it is fresh)
● 6 cups of warm water
● 4 teaspoons sugar
● 4 teaspoons salt
● 10–12 cups of plain flour

Note: *Before this activity you might like to make task cards for the children. This will make it easier for everybody to participate. You may want to set up two workstations and divide the children into two groups, one at each station. (In this case, make two sets of task cards and enlist a couple of parents or other adult helpers.) You will need to start this activity in the morning as it takes a few hours to complete.*

Steps
❶ *How many of you have/had bread in your lunches today?* Talk about different kinds of breads that the children like. (This is a good time for a survey on favourite breads or sandwiches, crust/no crust and so on. Compile, graph and display the results.)
❷ Before making the bread, demonstrate what happens to yeast when sugar is added. Do this by filling the two baby-food jars with warm water. Label one jar 'sugar' and the other 'no sugar'. Add a ½ sachet of yeast to each jar. Then add a pinch of sugar to the jar labelled 'sugar'. Ask the children to observe and describe what happens in both jars. (The yeast in the jar with sugar will foam up. The children will be able to smell the yeast). Explain that yeast plays an important role in making some kinds of bread. The reaction that they are observing is what helps bread dough to rise.

SCIENCE BACKGROUND
Yeast is classified as a fungus, a single-celled living organism. It cannot manufacture its own food like green plants can. In order for the yeast to grow, it has to be fed. This is why sugar is sometimes added to recipes that contain yeast. As the yeast feeds on the sugar, alcohol and carbon dioxide are formed. This reaction is called fermentation, and it is what makes bread dough rise. Yeast likes a warm environment, over 38°C. When making bread, this is best achieved by placing the dough in a warm place (like on a sunny windowsill) and covering it with a cloth.

VOCABULARY
fungus: a single-celled organism that, unlike green plants, does not make its own food

❸ Now tell the children that they must follow these steps to mix the bread dough. (These are the directions you can write on task cards.) Check that they all have clean hands!

● Measure ¼ cup of warm water into each of the bowls.

● Dissolve 2 teaspoons of sugar in each of the bowls.

● Add a sachet of yeast to both bowls. Stir to mix in the yeast, then let it sit for a couple of minutes. (Take a break for observations now and ask the children to describe what is happening. Within a minute you should start to see the yeast growing and bursting to the surface of the water.)

● Now add 2¾ cups of warm water to each bowl.

● Mix in 5–6 cups of flour and 2 teaspoons of salt to each bowl. (Add the flour a little at a time. The dough should be a little sticky.)

● Stir until the flour is mixed in well, then turn each piece of dough out onto the waxed paper.

● Coat hands with oil and knead each piece of dough for 10–15 minutes. Add a little more flour if the dough is too sticky to handle. (The children will have fun taking turns to do this.)

● Return the dough to clean, oiled bowls, using tape to mark the dough height on the outside of the bowls, and cover each with a cloth. Set one in a sunny windowsill and the second somewhere cool. (If your room is fairly warm, you may wish to put the second bowl of dough in a refrigerator). Ask the children to predict what they think will happen to the dough in both bowls. Then let the dough sit for about 1½ hours.

❹ After 1½ hours, check both bowls of dough. Let the children make observations and describe the dough. *How does the original height of each compare with the height now? Why do you think the dough in the sunny window grew but the other one stayed just about the same?* (Warmer temperatures increase yeast productivity.)

❺ Divide the dough that has risen in half. Let the children shape these halves into loaves. Place the loaves on an oiled baking sheet (or one sprinkled with flour), cover them with a cloth, and set them on the windowsill. Let them rise again until they double in size (about another hour).

❻ Bake the loaves at 180°C for about 45 minutes. When the bread is cooked it will sound hollow when it is tapped.

Assessing children's learning

Help the children to apply what they've learned about yeast, as well as review the sequence and process of bread-making, by finding a way to make the second bowl of bread dough rise. As the children discuss options, ask them to review their observation of both bowls. *What can you change to make the second bowl of dough rise?* (Place it in a warm spot.) After the dough rises, the children can use it to shape their own mini-loaves to bake. While the bread bakes, invite the children to write stories about their day baking bread. Encourage them to include details from their own experiences.

Tea and sunshine

On the day of the picnic, the children can explore infusion by making sun tea to drink. The Sun provides the warmth needed to make the flavour from the tea bags mix with the water.

Materials
- two clear 5-litre containers
- 20 herbal tea bags
- water
- lemon and sugar (optional)
- the children's science books
- writing and drawing materials

Steps

❶ Fill both containers with water and add ten tea bags to each one. Ask the children to observe the containers and draw what they see in their science books.

❷ Set one container on a sunny windowsill and one in a dark, cool place. Ask the children to predict what will happen in each container.

❸ Let the children check the containers after half an hour. *What do you notice?* Encourage them to record their new observations in their science books. (The water in the windowsill container will be more clearly infused with the colour of the tea than the water in the dark. If the children touch the containers, they will also find that the container on the windowsill is warmer.)

❹ Check again after a couple of hours and record observations. *How do the two containers compare with each other?* (The children will notice that the tea in the windowsill jar is more blended than the tea that was in the dark.)

❺ Now take the container that was in the dark, cool place and set it on the windowsill to speed up the infusion process. The children can serve both containers of tea at their picnic!

Window on child development

These activities invite the children to revisit many of the concepts introduced earlier in this book, including those related to light and heat ('The way light works', Chapter 5, and 'The Sun's warm ways', Chapter 6), evaporation and the water cycle ('Evaporation investigations', Chapter 4), seeds ('Sowing seeds', Chapter 7), and microscopic life ('Tiny worlds', Chapter 3). Revisiting concepts throughout the year gives children a chance to clear up misconceptions and allows them to build on their experiences to strengthen their understanding.

SCIENCE BACKGROUND
Tea is an example of an infusion – flavour is released from a substance soaked in water. When placed in water, the tea leaves begin to break apart, releasing flavour and colour into the water. The warmer the water, the more quickly the flavour and colour blend through it. This is because when the water is warmer, the water molecules move more quickly. This motion moves the dissolved tea through the water, helping to create an even mixture.

VOCABULARY
infusion: a liquid, like tea, that has acquired a flavour from a substance that has had hot water poured over it

Think about it

The children may already be asking questions like those that follow. The explanations are intended for your use, and the information may be adapted to suit the needs and development of your children.

Can you think of reasons why people dry food?

Dehydrated, or dried-out, food is used by astronauts and hikers (among others) because it is easy to pack, lightweight, and it doesn't go bad. Children who like raisins are also enjoying dried food.

Where does yeast come from?

Yeast is often found growing on fruits, where it can feed on the fruits' natural sugars. There are many different strains of yeast.

What are some ways that the Sun helps us?

The Sun provides us with light, which helps us to see things. Sunlight is also essential for plants to grow and to warm our planet. In fact, without the Sun life would not exist on our planet.

Extending the activities

- Find out what kinds of foods astronauts take into space.
- Do some research on the wide variety of breads that make up part of the diets of different peoples around the world.
- Investigate the health benefits of different kinds of foods and create sample healthy-meal menus. Plan and prepare one of the meals, inviting parents and carers to be your guests.

Resources

Books

Try to find one of a number of popular books that focus on a picnic to share at your own picnic. Two that are particularly suitable for young children are:

Mr Bear's Picnic by Debi Gliori (Orchard Books).

The Lighthouse Keeper's Picnic by Ronda and David Armitage (Scholastic).

Heinemann Library publish a range of books by Louise Spilsbury each examining one food, looking in particular at how it reaches our plates. They each include one recipe. See, for example, *Food: Bread.*